MEN WHO GOVERN

MEN WHO GOVERN

A Biographical Profile of Federal Political Executives

DAVID T. STANLEY

DEAN E. MANN

JAMESON W. DOIG

THE BROOKINGS INSTITUTION / WASHINGTON, D.C.

THE BROOKINGS INSTITUTION is an independent organization devoted to nonpartisan research, education, and publication in economics, government, foreign policy, and the social sciences generally. Its principal purposes are to aid in the development of sound public policies and to promote public understanding of issues of national importance.

The Institution was founded on December 8, 1927, to merge the activities of the Institute for Government Research, founded in 1916, the Institute of Economics, founded in 1922, and the Robert Brookings Graduate School of Economics and Government, founded in 1924.

The general administration of the Institution is the responsibility of a self-perpetuating Board of Trustees. The trustees are likewise charged with maintaining the independence of the staff and fostering the most favorable conditions for creative research and education. The immediate direction of the policies, program, and staff of the Institution is vested in the President, assisted by an advisory council chosen from the staff of the Institution.

In publishing a study, the Institution presents it as a competent treatment of a subject worthy of public consideration. The interpretations and conclusions in such publications are those of the author or authors and do not purport to represent the views of the other staff members, officers, or trustees of the Brookings Institution.

Foreword

PROBLEMS IN STAFFING high-level positions near the end of the Eisenhower administration focused renewed public attention on the process of selecting presidential appointees and on the qualifications and tenure of the persons chosen. The Brookings Institution took this occasion to start research on the appointments and backgrounds of federal political executives. The first product of this research was *The Assistant Secretaries: Problems and Processes of Appointment,* by Dean E. Mann, with Jameson W. Doig, published in 1965. The present study is a companion piece which analyzes the backgrounds, tenure in office, and subsequent careers of federal political executives from the beginning of the New Deal through the early years of the Johnson administration.

Mann and Doig made the initial plans for the study, collected and analyzed biographical information, and prepared first drafts of the findings. In 1964, under the direction of David T. Stanley, the coverage of the study was extended in time to cover the Johnson administration through April 1965 and extended in scope to cover seven regulatory commissions. Changes in the treatment and presentation of the statistical data were also made.

The study was conducted under the general guidance of George A. Graham, Director of Governmental Studies. Franklin P. Kilpatrick of the Governmental Studies senior staff gave valuable advice to the authors in the planning and execution of the project. Much of the detailed statistical work was done by Mrs. Virginia Baxter Benson, who also served as liaison with the data processors, National Analysts, Inc., of Philadelphia. Mrs. Jane O'Donnell, Sidney Binder, and Edwin E. Olson, all of National Analysts, provided valuable assistance. Secretarial work was performed by Mrs. Pamela Hanke, who also aided in data coding, and by Mrs. Jeanne B. Walker, Mrs. Loma Moore, Miss Deborah H. Bliss, and George B. Looney.

Significant data were contributed by the federal departments and agencies concerned and by the National Personnel Records Center, St. Louis, Missouri.

A major contribution by Dean Marver H. Bernstein of the Woodrow Wilson School of Public and International Affairs, Princeton University, is acknowledged with appreciation. He supplied extensive biographical data which he had collected on federal regulatory commissioners for the period 1936 to 1960.

The final manuscript was written by David Stanley, who received valuable advice from a reading committee consisting of Roger W. Jones, Herbert Kaufman, and Richard E. Neustadt, and from Dean Bernstein. The book was edited by Frances M. Shattuck and the index prepared by Helen Eisenhart.

The Institution is grateful for the special grant from the Carnegie Corporation that made it possible for Brookings to undertake this study and the companion study, *The Assistant Secretaries*. The Institution is also grateful to the Ford Foundation for the general support grant that has been drawn upon in completing this study.

The conclusions expressed are those of the authors and do not purport to represent the views of the trustees, the officers, or other staff members of the Brookings Institution or of the Carnegie Corporation or the Ford Foundation.

KERMIT GORDON
President

July 1967
Washington, D.C.

Contents

Charts

Appendix Tables

1

A Third of a Century, a Thousand Executives

ON APRIL 14, 1933, President Franklin D. Roosevelt appointed John Dickinson of Pennsylvania, a professor of political science and law, aged 39, as Assistant Secretary of Commerce.

Thirty-two years later President Lyndon B. Johnson appointed another 39 year-old Assistant Secretary of Commerce: Andrew F. Brimmer, an economist who had worked at the Federal Reserve Bank of New York, taught at several universities, and had served as Deputy Assistant Secretary.[1]

Between these two choices, the first white, the second Negro, five Presidents of the United States made nearly 1,600 other appointments in filling the 180 top federal positions discussed in this book. For these appointments the Presidents selected over 1,000 men, some of them more than once.[2] These were choices of crucial importance, for federal political executives occupy a uniquely influential position in American society. They make important decisions affecting commerce, agriculture, labor, and natural resources. They advise the President on decisions that he must make. They present and defend legislative recommendations before the Congress. They provide

---

[1] He later was made a member of the Board of Governors of the Federal Reserve System.

[2] See below, p. 8, for further detail on multiple appointments.

1

leadership for the civil service, the foreign service, and the military services.

The importance of these executives—and their quality—is recognized by the American people, as the results of another Brookings study show. Hundreds of citizens expressed their high regard for such federal appointees, commending their capability, integrity, and qualifications. Indeed, the more educated interviewees tended to give higher ratings to the appointees than to members of Congress (who were also rated high).[3]

This book is the second product of research on how federal political executives are recruited and chosen, and who they really are. The first was focused on the selection process.[4] Characterizing this process as "highly decentralized and personalized" and "pluralistic and inconsistent," the book nevertheless reported general satisfaction with its results on the part of both appointees and cabinet officers. Recommendations were made urging continued presidential participation in selections, provision of government experience for men from private life, and a number of steps to make executive positions more attractive.[5]

The present study concentrates on the personal and occupational characteristics of federal political executives appointed by five Presidents—Franklin D. Roosevelt, Harry S. Truman, Dwight D. Eisenhower, John F. Kennedy, and Lyndon B. Johnson. It includes the 108 persons covered in *The Assistant Secretaries* and goes further, both in the types of positions covered and in time. The total number is 1,041—all but twelve of them men. These executives came from all parts of the nation and a wide variety of occupations. Some had several university degrees; some had never gone to college. They held office for periods ranging from a few weeks to twenty-two years. Many are still on the job, others have gone on to new careers, and some have retired or died. Some were important political fig-

[3] For a preliminary presentation of these findings, see M. Kent Jennings, Milton C. Cummings, Jr., and Franklin P. Kilpatrick, "Trusted Leaders: Perceptions of Appointed Federal Officials," *Public Opinion Quarterly*, Vol. 30, (Fall 1966), pp. 368–84.

[4] Dean E. Mann with Jameson W. Doig, *The Assistant Secretaries: Problems and Processes of Appointment* (Brookings Institution, 1965).

[5] *Ibid.*, pp. 265–86.

ures; others were only nominal party members; and others were entirely inactive in politics.

This book sketches a profile of these men—where they came from; their ages, religions, politics; where they went to college; what they did before they were appointed; how long they held federal office; and what they did afterward. Parts of the profile (ages, religions, colleges attended) are less important for selection purposes than others (graduate training, length of previous federal service), yet all the findings contribute to an improved understanding of this important group.

Positions Studied

These executives include:

The secretaries, under secretaries, assistant secretaries, and general counsel of ten cabinet departments: State, Treasury, Defense, Justice, Post Office, Interior, Agriculture, Commerce, Labor, and Health, Education, and Welfare (Housing and Urban Development was established after completion of the research);

The same officials of the three military departments: Army, Navy, and Air Force;

The administrators and deputy administrators of selected major agencies: Agency for International Development, Bureau of the Budget, General Services Administration, Housing and Home Finance Agency, United States Information Agency, Veterans Administration, and the principal depression and war agencies;

Members of seven regulatory commissions and boards: Civil Aeronautics Board, Federal Communications Commission, Federal Power Commission, Federal Trade Commission, Interstate Commerce Commission, National Labor Relations Board, and Securities and Exchange Commission.

The period covered is from the beginning of the Franklin Roosevelt administration through the early Johnson appointments, to April 30, 1965.[6]

---

[6] See Appendix A for a detailed discussion of coverage and methodology, Appendix B for definition of terms.

There were 71 of these positions on March 4, 1933. The number grew with the New Deal, the rise of the depression agencies and the war agencies, and the growth of the federal government. When emergencies passed, positions were abolished or sometimes transferred; in the depression and war agencies, 28 were created and later disappeared. At the end of April 1965 there were 152 in existence.

Although these positions cover a broad range of vital functions, they do not represent the entire executive branch of government. Important public policies are developed, decided, or carried out by officials not included in the study, such as members of the Atomic Energy Commission, various assistants to the President, or members of the Council of Economic Advisers.

The positions held by the executives in this study are nearly all filled by presidential appointment with Senate confirmation. A few are selected by the President alone; a few others, by the department head concerned.

Over the years covered by the study the demands of these jobs have varied with the needs of the nation, the policies of the Presidents, the attitudes of Congress, the organization of the government, and many other factors. For the most part, the demands have grown. Budget Director Harold Smith developed a federal budget of some $9 billion for fiscal year 1940; this was less than one-tenth of the budget prepared by David Bell for fiscal year 1962. The responsibilities carried by Paul V. McNutt as Administrator of the Federal Security Agency from 1939 to 1945 were comprehensive, but they were modest compared with those of Anthony J. Celebrezze, Secretary of Health, Education, and Welfare in 1963.

The demands of some other jobs have diminished. Frank Knox as Secretary of the Navy in World War II was fully responsible for fleets waging a global war—obviously a more demanding assignment than those of Navy secretaries playing a supportive role in the 1960's to Secretary of Defense Robert McNamara. Followers have also had an easier job than trailbreakers. The task facing Joseph P. Kennedy as first chairman of the Securities and Exchange Commission was far more challenging than that facing his successors after precedents and regulations were established. A political executive also has an easier job if he takes office after his party has been in power for some years than if he has to direct a policy turnaround at a change of administration.

Thus there are vast qualitative differences among the same jobs from one period to another. There are equally great differences among the various executive positions in the same period of time. The Secretary of Defense, for example, makes procurement and manpower decisions involving billions of dollars and millions of citizens. The Secretary of Labor personally mediates disputes concerning details of work rules. A member of the Civil Aeronautics Board studies details of a fatal airplane accident. An assistant secretary of Health, Education, and Welfare reviews admission of Negro patients to hospitals. An assistant secretary of the Interior negotiates arrangements for water distribution among vast areas. The chairman of the Federal Power Commission investigates causes of a multistate power failure. The Interstate Commerce commissioners evaluate the proposed merger of two large railroads. The job requirements may be diplomatic, legal, statistical, economic, or sociological. Some executives are mainly deciders; some are advisers; some are facilitators; some must do all of these things.

The differences are even more extensive than these examples suggest. Each executive does many different kinds of work. The matters that claim his attention vary with the needs of the day, with his own personality and capabilities, with the wishes of his superiors, and with many other factors.

Despite these differences in job content, there are common elements. Most of these positions have high public visibility, political vulnerability, dynamic problems, and excessive work load. The executives must deal cogently and promptly with the White House staff, committees of Congress, individual politicians, career staff members, and clientele groups. They must spend much more time with people who say "no" and "why?" than with people who say "yes" or "good!" Above all, they must be synthesizers—able to get projects finished, decisions made, programs pushed ahead.[7]

---

[7] Among many discussions of political executive positions, see particularly: Mann, *The Assistant Secretaries*, pp. 2–4 and 191–220; Marver H. Bernstein, *The Job of the Federal Executive* (Brookings Institution, 1958), pp. 10–37; Commission on Organization of the Executive Branch of the Government, *Task Force Report on Personnel and Civil Service* (1955), pp. 39–48; Arthur

The companion volume to this one, *The Assistant Secretaries: Problems and Processes of Appointment*, portrays the selection process that has been used to meet the varying demands of these positions. Such a process is carried on through a great diversity of personal, economic, and political relationships. The recruitment process varies from one department to another, one administration to another, and even from one month to another, in the zeal and orderliness with which it is carried on.

The present study, covering more positions and a longer time span than its companion, sets forth the results of the selection process in terms of personal and occupational characteristics—what similarities and differences are there in the backgrounds and tenure of the men chosen to meet these high responsibilities?

Appointments: Presidents; Positions; Agencies

Roughly a quarter of the 1,567 executive appointments were made by President Roosevelt, another quarter by Truman, another by Eisenhower, and another by Kennedy and Johnson combined. Appendix Table C.1 shows the distribution by administration.

Normally a political executive served in the administration of only one President; this was true in 78 percent of the cases. It would be natural to expect carryover from Roosevelt to Truman, and 7 percent of the total did serve in both those administrations. Another 10 percent held office in both the Kennedy and Johnson administra-

---

W. Macmahon and John D. Millett, *Federal Administrators: A Biographical Approach to the Problem of Departmental Management* (Columbia University Press, 1939), pp. 155–303.

For material concerning commissioners, see: E. Pendleton Herring, *Federal Commissioners* (Harvard University Press, 1936); Marver H. Bernstein, *Regulating Business by Independent Commission* (Princeton University Press, 1955), esp. pp. 103–25.

For comparative data about permanent secretaries in Great Britain, see: John S. Harris and Thomas V. Garcia, "The Permanent Secretaries: Britain's Top Administrators," *Public Administration Review*, Vol. 26 (March 1966), pp. 31–44.

tions; and the remaining 5 percent served in the other combinations of presidencies.

As to the jobs they held, there were far more appointments to assistant secretary positions than to any others, as shown in Table 1.1.

TABLE 1.1. *Number of Appointments, by Position Level* [a]

	Appointments	
Position Level	Number	*Percentage of Total*
Cabinet secretary	99	*6%*
Military secretary	24	*2*
Under secretary	172	*11*
Assistant secretary	613	*39*
General counsel	106	*7*
Administrator	95	*6*
Deputy administrator	123	*8*
Commissioner	335	*21*
Total	1,567	*100%*

[a] Appointments by administration and position level are shown in Appendix Table C.1.

The number of these appointments made to each department depended partly upon its organization and partly upon its customary personnel practices. The largest number of federal political executive appointments, as defined in this study, was 182 in the Department of State, which had (as of April 30, 1965) two deputy under secretaries and ten assistant secretaries and a tradition of rotating officials from one position to another. Second, with 139, was the Department of Justice, with its nine assistant attorney general positions. Farther down in the scale were the Departments of Labor (59 appointments) and Agriculture (54). In both there are relatively few political executive positions, and the appointees stayed in the positions longer.[8] (See Appendix Table C.2 for appointments distributed by administration and agency.)

[8] Tenure is discussed in Chap. 4.

Multiple Appointments

One man–one appointment was a general but far from invariable rule. Three out of every eight persons studied had more than one appointment.[9] Dean Acheson, for example, had four: Under Secretary of the Treasury and Assistant Secretary, Under Secretary, and Secretary of State. Robert B. Anderson had three: Secretary of the Navy, Deputy Secretary of Defense, and Secretary of the Treasury. Cyrus Vance was appointed General Counsel at Defense, then Secretary of the Army, then Deputy Secretary of Defense. The late James M. Landis was appointed to three different regulatory bodies: the Federal Trade Commission, the Securities and Exchange Commission, and the Civil Aeronautics Board. These examples are exceptional, for only 11 percent of the executives had more than two appointments. (See Appendix Table C.3 for more detail.) However, because some did receive two or more appointments to federal executive positions, the statistical material deals part of the time with the 1,041 persons and at other times with the 1,567 appointments they held; this is especially the case in Chapter 3.

The general rule was also one man–one agency. Nine out of ten executives (91 percent) served in only one agency; 7 percent, in only two; 1 percent served in three.[10] Thus political executives are far less likely to cross agency lines than are high federal civil servants, 56 percent of whom worked in one agency, 30 percent in two, and 9 percent in three.[11] It would be natural to expect more mobility in the civil service, where tenure is much longer and where movement to another agency may be necessary for career progress.

With these dimensions of the group identified, it is time to move on to more detailed analysis of these thousand-plus executives. Where did they come from? How were they educated? What were their occupations? How long did they serve as political executives? What later careers did they follow?

[9] See definition of appointments in Appendix B. Observe especially that an executive (other than a commissioner) whose service continues more than six months into a new presidency is considered to have been reappointed. Reappointments of commissioners are discussed in Chap. 4.

[10] Percentages do not add to 100 because of rounding.

[11] David T. Stanley, *The Higher Civil Service* (Brookings Institution, 1964), p. 33. The remainder worked in four to six agencies.

2

Personal Backgrounds

THESE ONE THOUSAND EXECUTIVES represent all sections of the country, all sizes of communities, and all levels of education above high school; but there are clear concentrations in the five administrations covered here—concentrations of men from the East, the big cities, and the better known colleges. There are high proportions also of Protestants, and of men in their late forties or early fifties.

Geographic Origins

The question "Where are they from?" has been answered by listing the location of each executive's principal occupation before appointment. This is a more realistic geographical indicator than two others which might have been used: birthplace or legal residence. Early work on this study showed that federal political executives tend to move away from their places of birth. Their mobility, like that of leaders in business, is away from farms and small towns and toward cities, especially those in the East.[1] Appendix Table D.1 shows how the percentages of executives from the census regions change when a comparison is made of their birthplaces, their legal

---

[1] See W. Lloyd Warner and James C. Abegglen, *Big Business Leaders in America* (Harper, 1955), pp. 177–96; and W. Lloyd Warner, Paul P. Van Riper, Norman H. Martin, and Orvis F. Collins, *The American Federal Executive* (Yale University Press, 1963), pp. 39–55.

residences, and the location of their principal occupations prior to appointment. Since the emphasis of the present study is more occupational than demographic or sociological, it was decided to show the locations where the men spent the more important part of their careers. Legal residence was not used because people in or near politics have been known to choose their "legal" states of residence on the basis of political factors rather than on the basis of where they have worked most of the time.

Such analysis of work locations shows that more than half of these federal political executives were from the Middle Atlantic and South Atlantic census regions (Chart 2.1). The areas that produced less than their "fair share" of executives, compared with the total population (as of the 1950 census), were mainly in a broad band down the center of the country: from North Dakota to Ohio, from Texas to Mississippi.[2] The West Coast was slightly underrepresented. The region most grossly overrepresented was the South Atlantic, because it includes Washington, D. C., residence of many executives who had been serving in lower political jobs or career jobs in the government (Chapter 3); but if Washington is excluded from the South Atlantic figures, that region is a relatively poor source. The remaining regions produced federal political executives in proportion to their population.

This geographical pattern prevails in all five presidencies, with a few variations (Appendix Table D.2). Presidents Truman and Johnson, both of whom inherited administrations, appointed or reappointed so many executives who had long been working in the government that the Washington disproportion became even greater. President Eisenhower treated the Republican Midwest and the Plains states better than the Democratic Presidents—recall his appointments of Ohioan George Humphrey as Secretary of the Treasury and Nebraska's Fred Seaton as Secretary of the Interior. Also, as incoming leader of a party long out of power, he naturally deflated the Washington bulge. The New England contingent was high under Harvard graduate Roosevelt and grew again under that region's native son, President Kennedy. Finally, there was a steady

---

[2] That is, the West North Central, East North Central, West South Central, and East South Central census regions.

CHART 2.1. *Location by Census Region of Principal Occupations Before Appointment, Compared with U. S. Population*

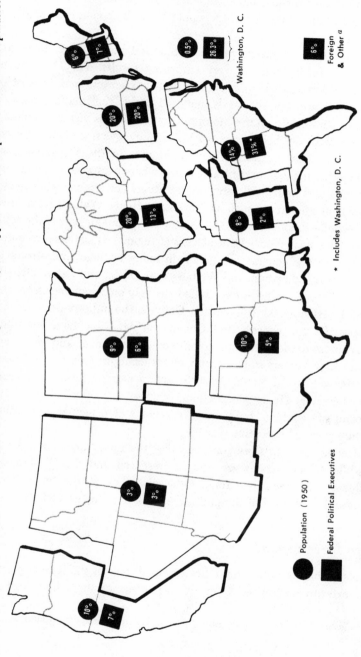

Population (1950)

Federal Political Executives

* Includes Washington, D. C.

ᵃ This category, not matched in the census data, is comprised of executives whose principal occupation before appointment was overseas or in military service.

11

climb in the Pacific Coast representation, reflecting increasing political attention to the growing population and economic strength of
that area.

When the geographic regions are sorted by agencies, there are
some interesting but not very surprising results. The Department
of the Interior, with its programs and its clientele mainly west of
the Mississippi—public lands, national parks, reclamation, mines—
has drawn heavily on the Mountain states and has virtually ignored
the East.[3] Under Secretary John J. Dempsey was from New Mexico,
Secretary Oscar Chapman from Colorado. In the Department of
Agriculture the various central regions—where prosperous agriculture
abounds and influential farm organizations are strong—were heavy
sources of executives, such as Secretaries Henry Wallace from Iowa
and Orville Freeman from Minnesota. The populous part of the Midwest (the East North Central census region) is underrepresented
relative to the general population in many agencies but strong in
the Health, Education, and Welfare, Post Office, and Labor Departments. Several agencies have relied strongly on appointees from the
Middle Atlantic states: Treasury, Defense, the military departments
(especially Air Force), and Commerce. All these have recruited
heavily from the world of commerce and finance, and there are
many New Yorkers in this group, as for example, Commerce Under
Secretary Edward Noble, Army Secretary Stanley Resor, and Treasury Secretary Henry Morgenthau, Jr. (See Appendix Table D.3 for
a complete analysis, by agency, of regions of principal occupation
before political executive service.)

Among the regulatory commissioners the East North Central and
Middle Atlantic states are underrepresented and the Washington
influence is especially strong. Otherwise they follow the general
geographic patterns of the political executive group as a whole.

How Large a Town?

New York and other big cities supplied most of the federal political executives studied. Over three-quarters of them had worked

---

[3] Except for the heavy Washington, D. C., representation, found in all
agencies.

primarily in cities with populations of 100,000 or more, while the 1950 census showed that about one-quarter of the general population was located in such cities (Chart 2.2.). Only 11 percent of the executives had been in communities of under 25,000, although about 60 percent of the general population lived in these smaller localities. Washington, where so many political executives had worked in other capacities, supplied 28 percent of them (though that city had only 0.5 percent of the United States population in 1950). New York, with 5 percent of the population, supplied 15 percent of the federal political executives.

The appointment patterns of the five Presidents differ in some details. Eisenhower was the best patron of both the small-towners and of executives from cities of over 100,000, except Washington and New York. Roosevelt and Johnson appointed the most men from towns

CHART 2.2. *Size of City of Principal Occupations Before Appointment, Compared with United States Population*

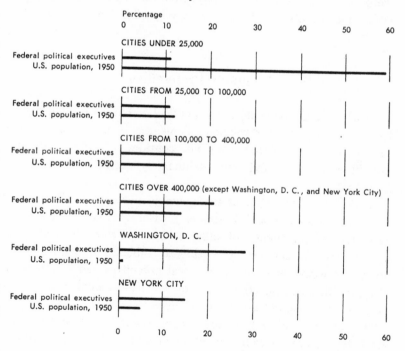

of 25,000 to 100,000. The hold-over Presidents, Truman and Johnson, as noted earlier, were the largest users of Washington talent. (See Appendix Table D.4 for figures in more detail.)

When the size-of-town figures were studied by agencies, the Post Office and Health, Education, and Welfare Departments seemed most like the general government pattern. Interior and Agriculture drew heavily from communities of under 100,000, as might be expected. Washington, D. C., supplied the highest proportion of executives in the State Department, Agriculture, and the regulatory commissions (except the Federal Power and Interstate Commerce Commissions). The heavy users of New York City talent were Army, Air Force, Treasury, Securities and Exchange Commission, Commerce, State, and Defense, in that order. Representatives of big cities other than New York and Washington were found in greatest concentration in Justice, Defense, Navy, Labor, Commerce, Post Office, and SEC. (See Appendix Table D.5 for detailed figures by agencies.)

Federal political executives, then, during this third of a century were preponderantly "big city boys from the East." While this generalization is gross, and to some it may be offensive, it is true.

Religious Preferences

Nearly half (44 percent) of the political executives did not supply information about their religions. Some are doubtless among the unchurched; some probably did not consider this information important or relevant; and some deliberately decided not to reveal their preferences.

Of the 578 whose religions are known, 77 percent were Protestant, 19 percent Catholic, and 4 percent Jewish. This large majority of Protestants is consistent with other evidence of their domination of various types of American leadership, as Table 2.1 shows. Catholics are better represented among political executives and members of Congress than among other types of leaders—although not in proportion to the overall Catholic population.

Two churches of high socioeconomic status, the Episcopal and Presbyterian, are overrepresented, compared with the population.

TABLE 2.1. *Religious Preferences of Federal Political Executives, Compared with United States Church Membership, Business Executives, Congress, and Military Leaders* [a]

Religion	Federal Political Executives	U.S. Church Membership 1958 [b]	Business Executives 1950 [c]	87th Congress [d]		Military Leaders, 1950 [e]		
				Senate	House	Army	Navy	Air Force
Roman Catholic	19%	36%	9%	12%	21%	11%	10%	16%
Jewish	4	5	5	1	3	—	—	—
Protestant (total)	77	56	f	87 [a]	77 [a]	89	90	84
Episcopal	25	3	30	13	12	g	g	g
Presbyterian	17	4	23	11	14	g	g	g
Methodist	11	11	10	19	18	g	g	g
Baptist	5	19	6	13	11	g	g	g
Congregational [h]	5	1	7	7	4	g	g	g
Other or unspecified	14	18	11 [f]	22	17	g	g	g
Other	—	3	f	—	—	g	g	g
Number of persons	578	b	390	98	429	166	205	106

[a] Percentages for subtotals may not add to 100 (or to Protestant subtotal) because of rounding.
[b] Compiled from church membership statistics in *Yearbook of American Churches for 1960* (National Council of the Churches of Christ in the U. S. A.), pp. 252-58. Total membership was about 110,000,000.
[c] Mabel Newcomer, *The Big Business Executive* (Columbia University Press, 1955), p. 48.
[d] As of March 22, 1961; derived from data in *Congressional Quarterly Almanac*, Vol. 17 (1961), p. 36.
[e] Morris Janowitz, *The Professional Soldier* (The Free Press, 1960), p. 98.
[f] "Other" for this column includes some Protestant faiths, so there are no figures for total Protestant or other or unspecified Protestant.
[g] No data for specific Protestant sects.
[h] Congregational Christian Church only, before its merger with Evangelical and Reformed Churches in 1957 to become United Church of Christ.

Baptists, who are more numerous in lower socioeconomic groups, are underrepresented in leadership positions.[4]

In view of the traditional Catholic and Jewish preferences for the Democratic party, it is not surprising that both faiths are better represented in the Democratic administrations, as shown in the following table:

ADMINISTRATION	PROTESTANT	CATHOLIC	JEWISH
All five	77%	19%	4%
Roosevelt	79	18	3
Truman	74	20	6
Eisenhower	85	14	1
Kennedy	67	26	7
Johnson	61	33	6

An increased acceptance of Catholics in leadership posts is shown by the much larger proportion of members of that faith in the Kennedy and Johnson administrations.

Religious preferences were not tabulated by position and agency for the full period 1933–65. Preliminary figures early in the study, however, suggested that there were no significant religious differences among position levels. The early figures did show, however, a disproportionately high number of Catholics in the Justice, Labor, and Post Office Departments and of Episcopalians in Treasury and State.

When the regulatory commissioners' religious affiliations are compared with those studied earlier by Pendleton Herring, there are some differences. The Catholic representation doubled (8 percent in the Herring study, 16 percent in this one), the proportion of Jews rose from 1 to 3 percent and the Protestant commissioners declined from 91 to 81 percent. Among the Protestant denominations, the largest difference was among the Presbyterians—Herring 29 percent, Brookings 20 percent.[5]

[4] See Nicholas J. Demerath, *Social Class in American Protestantism* (Rand McNally, 1965), pp. 2–3.

[5] E. Pendleton Herring, *Federal Commissioners* (Harvard University Press, 1936), p. 111. The commissions studied do not coincide with those in the present study. Herring covers three commissions included in the present study (FPC, FTC, and ICC) and three not included (Federal Radio Commission, Federal Reserve Board, and U. S. Tariff Commission).

Education

Federal political executives, like many other leaders in American society, have been extremely well educated, compared with the general population. Like other leadership groups, too, they show a rising trend in educational level over the period studied. Of the total number, 93 percent attended college. The size of the college group increased steadily from 88 percent in the Roosevelt administration tò 99 percent in the Johnson administration.

Three out of every four had college degrees, and 68 percent had done some graduate work. Seventeen percent had earned master's degrees, and 11 percent doctorates. Men with legal training were abundant: 44 percent had received a primary law degree (LL.B. or J.D.), some in lieu of a bachelor's degree, others in addition to it.

The educational levels of recent federal political executives are strikingly higher than those of the general population and well above those of other leadership groups (Table 2.2.). In all such groups it would be natural to expect a rising educational level over a period of time. Among the federal political executives such a trend from one presidency to another is shown in Chart 2.3.

Further evidence of this increase in educational level is found in a comparison of Herring's study of earlier commissioners with the present study. Of the group studied by Herring, 84 percent had gone to college, as compared with 93 percent of those in the present study.[6]

A similar trend is found among presidents of leading business corporations. Here the percentage of college graduates rose from 70 to 83 during the years 1954–64. In the same period the proportion of those who had done graduate work rose from one in five to one in three.[7]

---

[6] Herring, *Federal Commissioners*, p. 109 (subject to the differences in coverage indicated in note 5, p. 16).

[7] William C. Hanneman and Thomas W. Harrell, "Changing Characteristics of Corporate Presidents," *Personnel*, Vol. 41 (September-October 1964), p. 52. Another study of corporate executives showed a like trend when "older" and "younger" executives were compared in 1950 and in 1964; *The Big Business Executive/1964*, p. 34.

TABLE 2.2. *Educational Levels of Recent Federal Political Executives, Compared with Other Groups* [a]

| Group | Date of Information | Educational Level | | | Number of Persons |
		No College	Some College, No Degree	College Degree	
U.S. adult white population, over age 25	1960	*83%*	*9%*	*8%*	89.6 million
Federal political executives	1961-1965	*2*	*5*	*93*	*232*
Big business executives [b]	1964	*9*	*16*	*74*	990
Top federal civil servants [c]	1963	*4*	*13*	*83*	*555*
California state government executives [d]	1965	. . .	. . .	*75*	1,227
Random sample, *Who's Who* [b]	1963	*6*	*12*	*83*	not given
U.S. Senators [e]	1964	*4*	*13*	*83*	100
U.S. Representatives [e]	1964	*7*	*14*	*79*	435

[a] Percentages may not add to 100 because of rounding.

[b] *The Big Business Executive/1964* (Scientific American, Inc., 1965), p. 36.

[c] David T. Stanley, *The Higher Civil Service* (Brookings Institution, 1964), pp. 30, 138.

[d] Commission on California State Government Organization and Economy, *A Study of Management Manpower Requirements, California State Government* (1965), p. 17.

[e] *Congressional Directory*, 88 Cong. 2 sess. (1964), and *Biographical Directory of the American Congress, 1774-1961* (1961).

Educational levels among federal political executives differ very little from one type of position to another (Appendix Table D.6). Those with legal training were numerous—44 percent of the entire group. Law degrees were especially plentiful among the military department secretaries, the regulatory commissioners, and (naturally) general counsel. The cabinet officers and military secretaries were less likely to have doctor's degrees; this may reflect the use of generalists and lawyers in such positions, rather than specialists with Ph.D's. The lowest proportions of college graduates were among cabinet secretaries and deputy administrators: 70 and 72 percent, respectively, compared with 76 percent for all the executives.

Distinctive patterns emerge when educational levels are compared across department and agency lines (Appendix Table D.7). Departments concerned with foreign relations, defense, and finance have

CHART 2.3. *Level of Education, by Administration*

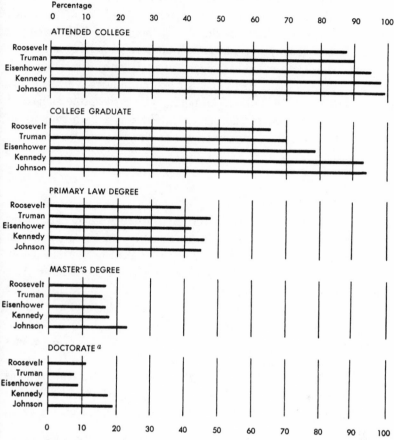

Note: Categories of graduate degrees are not mutually exclusive. A person is counted once for each type of degree he holds.

ᵃ Does not include honorary degrees.

the highest proportions of college graduates. For example, State has 83 percent; Treasury, 87 percent; Defense, 84 percent; Army, 90 percent; Air Force, 91 percent. The Department of Health, Education, and Welfare is also understandably high—85 percent.[8] Post

[8] The high figures for HEW, Defense, and Air Force are partly explained by the fact that these departments were created later than 1933 (HEW's predecessor, Federal Security Agency, in 1939, and Defense and Air Force in 1947). It has already been shown that educational levels rose through the period covered by this study.

Office and Labor, with a significant number of their executives from clerical and blue-collar backgrounds, have the lowest percentages of college graduates: 50 and 68 percent, respectively. Agriculture and Air Force lead the parade of Ph.D's (29 percent and 17 percent). The highest concentrations of master's degrees are among the social workers, educators, and other specialists of Health, Education, and Welfare (26 percent), the economists and administrative specialists of the Bureau of the Budget (38 percent), and the professionals of the Department of State (25 percent). There is a high proportion of lawyers among the commissioners—59 percent with primary law degrees.

Which Schools and Colleges?

PRIVATE SCHOOLS. Another characteristic of these political executives, compared with the general public, is that they were more likely to go to private secondary schools.[9] Even though data were available for only a little more than half the group, the picture is clear. At a time when only 6 or 7 percent of the United States population went to private schools, over 20 percent of these 1,041 future federal executives did so.[10] This proportion compares with 15 percent of United States senators and 28 percent of the presidents of America's largest corporations who attended private schools.[11]

Nearly half of the political executives who went to private schools attended one or more of eighteen "name" prep schools in the East: Avon Old Farms, Choate, Deerfield, Groton, Hill, Hotchkiss, Kent,

[9] Private secondary schools include religious schools; available information did not make it possible to make a complete separation of Catholic and other religious academies from secular private schools. Eighteen "name" secular private schools are, however, tabulated separately below.

[10] 6.9 percent of secondary school pupils in 1930 went to private schools (U. S. Bureau of the Census, *Statistical Abstract of the United States: 1940*, p. 113); and 6.4 percent in 1940 (*Statistical Abstract . . . 1942*, p. 140). Percentages shown for federal political executives are based on the total group studied (1,041 persons); only 550 of them recorded data in *Who's Who* or other biographical sources concerning their secondary education. It is assumed that nearly all of the remaining 491 attended public schools.

[11] Andrew Hacker, "The Elected and the Anointed: Two American Elites," *American Political Science Review*, Vol. 55 (September 1961), p. 541. Data are based on positions held in 1959.

Lawrenceville, Loomis, Middlesex, Milton, Phillips Andover, Phillips Exeter, St. George's, St. Mark's, St. Paul's, Taft, and Thatcher.

From one administration to another, there was little variation in the proportion who attended private schools. Eisenhower, Kennedy, and Johnson appointed the highest percentages of "name" prep school men, while President Eisenhower appointed the largest share of persons who had attended all types of private schools (Appendix Table D.8).

There were wide differences among departments and agencies in their executives' precollege education. The same departments which were high in percentages of college graduates (State, Treasury, Defense, Army, Navy) were also those with high percentages of "name" school alumni and total private school alumni. The lowest departments in these respects were Interior and Agriculture. Among the regulatory commissions, the Securities and Exchange Commission, Federal Trade Commission, and Civil Aeronautics Board were high in percentages of commissioners who had gone to private schools. Interstate Commerce and the National Labor Relations Board were low, and the Federal Power Commission was manned entirely by public school men during the period under study. (See Appendix Table D.9 for details.)

In general, these figures are further impressive evidence that federal political executives tend to be selected from a high socio-economic group.

UNDERGRADUATE COLLEGES. Ranking of colleges and universities attended showed an impressive concentration of well-known institutions (Appendix Table D.10). The "Big Three" (Yale, Harvard, and Princeton) and the Ivy League[12] generally led the list. One out of every four executives was an Ivy League man, and the "Big Three" accounted for one out of every five. Yale ranked first in every administration except President Eisenhower's, and was in second place then behind Harvard. The Ivy influence was at its peak under Eisenhower —resulting in part from his use of members of the New York business community as recruiters. Some of the leading state universities were also major producers of federal political executives. There was

[12] Brown, Columbia, Cornell, Dartmouth, Harvard, Pennsylvania, Princeton, and Yale.

little variation in the rank of the institutions from one administration to another.

From 1933 to 1965 the government drew 40 percent of political executives from the top eighteen institutions tabulated for this study, and the proportion was greater in the last three administrations than in the first two. These institutions supplied 36 percent of Roosevelt's appointees and 37 percent of Truman's. There was a sharp rise to 47 percent under Eisenhower, followed by a leveling-off—Kennedy 44 percent, and Johnson 45 percent.

The colleges most frequently attended by political executives tend to be among those ranked among the nation's most selective in a recent study:

Six (Chicago, Columbia, Dartmouth, Harvard, Princeton, and Yale) are among the nineteen "most selective" colleges;

Two (Cornell and Stanford) are among the forty-one "highly selective" colleges;

Three (California-Berkeley, Michigan, and North Carolina) are among the one hundred twenty-one "very selective" colleges;

Two (Northwestern and Texas) are among the one hundred fifty-eight "selective" colleges.[13]

A similar concentration in well-known institutions is also found among big business executives, according to several studies. Among the corporate presidents described by Hanneman and Harrell, for example, about one in five had attended Ivy League colleges: 17 percent of 1950–52 presidents; 23 percent of 1961–63 presidents.[14] When the leading institutions attended by political and business executives are ranked, as in Appendix Table D.11, the same names recur frequently, particularly Harvard, Princeton, and Yale. Other familiar institutions are fairly constant sources: Columbia, Cornell,

[13] James Cass and Max Birnbaum, *Comparative Guide to American Colleges* (Harper and Row, 1964), pp. 526–28. The authors say this about the selectivity categories: "These categories are general, but they are based on statistical and other factual information: the percentage of applicants accepted by the college, the average test scores of recent freshman classes, the ranking of recent freshmen in their high school classes, and other related data which measure the scholastic potential of the student body" (p. xii).

[14] Hanneman and Harrell, in *Personnel*, p. 53.

015282

Dartmouth, and Pennsylvania from the Ivy League; and Chicago, Massachusetts Institute of Technology, Michigan, and Wisconsin.[15]

GRADUATE EDUCATION. About two-thirds of the political executives attended graduate schools, and the better known, larger universities are again prominent in the count (Appendix Table D.12). Because of the large number of executives with law degrees, figures are shown separately for the lawyers and non-lawyers. Either way, Harvard tops the list, with 22 percent of those with law degrees and 17 percent of those with non-law graduate degrees. Yale is second for those with legal degrees; Columbia, for those without. Other familiar state and private universities are also prominent. Three institutions are of special interest: George Washington and Georgetown, where the men went to night classes in Washington,[16] and Oxford, where twenty-five executives studied as Rhodes Scholars and ten others also took graduate work.

The graduate schools most frequently attended by executives tend to be among those rated highly in the quality of their doctoral programs in social sciences and humanities by a recent study of the American Council on Education (Table 2.3).

Political Affiliation and Activity

Under our political system a President is expected to appoint members of his own party to the top executive positions. It is not surprising, then, that Democratic appointees far outnumbered Republicans during a period in which there were four Democratic Presidents in office for twenty-four years, as against one Republican President for eight. Yet all five appointed members of the opposing party to office, either to gain bipartisan support for certain policies, or to get an appointee with particularly high qualifications. Examples include President Kennedy's appointments of Douglas Dillon as Secretary of the Treasury and Robert McNamara as Secretary of

[15] For further strong evidence on the relationship between attendance at prestige universities and success in business (this time in terms of directorships in large corporations), see Stanley C. Vance, "Higher Education for the Executive Elite," *California Management Review*, Vol. 8 (Summer 1966), pp. 21–30.

[16] Mostly before they became political executives.

TABLE 2.3. *Rankings of Graduate Schools in Social Sciences and Humanities, Compared with Those Attended by Largest Numbers of Federal Political Executives*

University	Quality of Social Sciences Doctoral Program [a]	Quality of Humanities Doctoral Program [a]	Attendance by Federal Political Executives With Graduate Degrees but No Law Degree
Harvard	1	1	1
California (Berkeley)	2	2	6
Chicago	3	b	3
Yale	4	3	8
Princeton	5	4	9
Wisconsin	6	b	7
Columbia	7	5	2
Michigan	8	6	4
Stanford	9	b	12

   [a] Allan M. Cartter, *An Assessment of Quality in Graduate Education* (American Council on Education, 1966), p. 107. Comparisons were not made with ratings of programs in engineering and the natural sciences because of the relatively small numbers of political executives educated in those fields.
   [b] Only top six ranked.

Defense. About 8 percent of the appointees were members of the party opposing the President. All five also appointed a substantial number (over one out of every four) of executives who were neither Democratic nor Republican partisans. The appointment picture for the five administrations is shown in Table 2.4. Commissioners were

TABLE 2.4. *Political Party Affiliation, by Administration* [a]

Administration	Number of Appointments			Political Affiliation		
	Total	No Data	Data Available	Demo-cratic	Repub-lican	Other or "None"
All five	1,232	328	904	57%	33%	10%
Roosevelt	245	78	167	89	10	1
Truman	314	108	206	84	13	4
Eisenhower	351	38	313	5	76	20
Kennedy	178	51	127	81	9	9
Johnson	144	53	91	84	8	9

   [a] Percentages may not add to 100 because of rounding. This table excludes commissioners (see discussion in text).

excluded, since the table is intended to show a free choice among parties and six of the regulatory commissions operate under laws containing such language as "no more than [a bare majority] of members may be of the same political party." The seventh, the National Labor Relations Board, is bipartisan, not by law but by fairly recent custom; Presidents beginning with Eisenhower have have maintained a 3-to-2 split, with the President's party in the majority. Thus in all seven bodies the President is almost sure to appoint a majority from his own party and a minority from the other.

In reviewing the figures the reader should again recall that holdovers of more than six months from the previous administration are counted as appointments. President Roosevelt appointed the highest percentage of executives from his own party. President Eisenhower appointed the lowest percentage from his own party—and the lowest from the opposing party, as well—because he selected so many independents. The commissioners, for the reason noted earlier, were least likely to be without political affiliation. Unaffiliated cabinet officers were also very few. The deputy administrators, assistant secretaries, and general counsel were the positions most frequently filled by men whose political affiliation was not solidly recorded as either Democratic or Republican. Undoubtedly some of these were former career government employees who had taken pains to remain politically anonymous.

The positions most frequently filled from the opposing party were the most visible ones—cabinet officers—thus strengthening the view that this is done to gain both quality and bipartisan support—usually businessmen's support of a Democratic administration. Least likely to be filled from the opposition were the general counsel positions.

Political affiliations were not analyzed by agency for the entire group studied. In the early phases of the research, covering 1933 through the first round of Kennedy appointments, two patterns were clear: Appointments from the opposition party were much more likely to be made to agencies concerned with foreign relations and defense than to other agencies, particularly Agriculture and Post Office; appointments were just as likely to be partisan in the later phases of a presidency as at the beginning.

Two forms of political activity were also analyzed in the early phase of this research project: attending national party conventions

2626 MEN WHO GOVERN

and making large campaign contributions ($500 or more). In both respects a few of the men selected to be political executives had been active. About 14 percent of the appointees had been convention delegates, and the same percentage had made large campaign contributions. Convention attendance varied by agencies. Nearly one out of four—23 percent—of Post Office executives had been delegates, and 27 percent of those in Interior had seen such service. The departments concerned with foreign relations and defense averaged under 10 percent, except for Navy, where 20 percent of the executives had attended conventions.

Age When Appointed

Federal political executives, like many other executives and politicians, generally arrived at these vocational peaks in their late forties and early fifties. Those in the Truman administration were youngest (median 46), even younger than Kennedy appointees (47), while the Eisenhower men were the oldest (51). All four Democratic administrations appointed younger executives than the Republican regime, which may suggest that persons of consequence within the Grand Old Party tend to be older than their adversaries. All in all, however, the five-year span is a narrow one, and it is not unreasonable to consider the Truman "46's" and the Eisenhower "51's" in the same age group. (See Chart 2.4 for comparative distributions.) The overall median age was 48.[17]

In contacts with top civil servants and with congressmen, the political executives find themselves dealing with close contemporaries. Table 2.5 shows age distributions and medians for higher civil servants, United States senators, and representatives, as well as for political executives. The senators tend to be older.

[17] The figures from which the medians were derived were computed on different bases. The "by administration" figure reflects the age at which the person was first appointed to a political executive position in a particular administration. The "by position level" figure concerns the age at which the person was first appointed to a political executive position of a certain level (for example, assistant secretary). The overall median reflects the age at which the person was first appointed to any political executive position.

CHART 2.4. *Distribution of Ages at Appointment, by Administration*

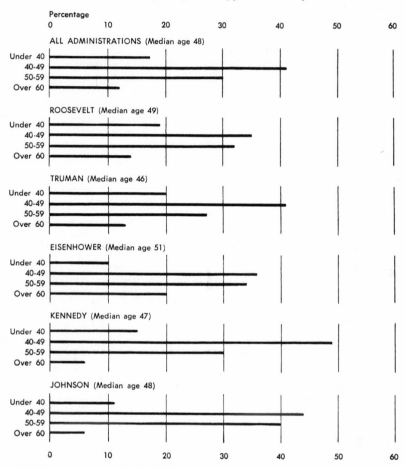

Note: Percentages may not add to 100 because of rounding.

Numbers of persons in individual administrations do not add to the total for all administrations, because a person is counted once in each administration he served, but only once in the total for all five administrations.

Presidents of large corporations are in the same age group, too.[18] Those appointed in 1961–63 to head corporations averaged 51 years of age, and those appointed in 1950–52 over 53, according to one

[18] Thus reducing opportunities to use such terms as "fogey" or "whipper-snapper" on occasions when business-government relations deteriorate.

TABLE 2.5.   *Ages at Appointment of Federal Political Executives, Compared with High Civil Servants, Senators, and Representatives* [a]

Category	Date	Age				Median Age	Number of Persons
		30's and Under	40's	50's	60's and Over		
Federal political executives [b]	1933-1965	17%	41%	30%	12%	48 [c]	1,010
Higher civil servants [d]	1962-1965	12	42	33	13	49 [e]	556
Representatives [f]	1963	11	35	30	24	51 [e]	434
Senators [f]	1963	6	17	35	41	57 [e]	99

[a] Percentages may not add to 100 because of rounding.
[b] Age at first appointment to political executive position.
[c] Medians for this study, in this and subsequent tables, are ungrouped unless specifically stated otherwise.
[d] Age at which highest civil service grade reached was first shown on personnel record. Source: Stanley, *Higher Civil Service*, pp. 35-36.
[e] Grouped median.
[f] Age in 1963. Source: *Congressional Quarterly Almanac*, Vol. 19 (1963), pp. 33-37.

study.[19] Other sources show a median age of 52 for men attaining top executive positions in industry in 1950, and a median of 50 for those reaching the top in 1964.[20]

Department and agency heads naturally tended to be older than the other executives: cabinet secretaries, military secretaries, and administrators were more likely to be in their fifties when appointed, while the others were more likely to take office in their forties. The general counsel were clearly the youngest group (median age 44), followed by assistant secretaries (46). (See Appendix Table D.13 for a distribution of ages by position level and Appendix Table D.14 for a tabulation of median ages by position level and administration.)

In any one position level there were wide variations. Averell Harriman was 70 when President Kennedy made him Assistant Secretary of State, and Richard Murphy was 31 when JFK appointed him Assistant Postmaster General. Among commissioners, James Landis was 34 when President Roosevelt appointed him to the Securities and Exchange Commission, and Clyde B. Atchison was 74

[19] Hanneman and Harrell, in *Personnel*, p. 53.
[20] Mabel Newcomer, *The Big Business Executive* (Columbia University Press, 1955), Table 30, p. 78; and *The Big Business Executive/1964*, p. 43.

when he was reappointed to the Interstate Commerce Commission by President Truman. Under secretaries and assistant secretaries appointed from 1933 to 1965 were generally *older* than those appointed in earlier periods, judging by data recorded by Macmahon and Millett. (Table 2.6).

TABLE 2.6.   *Comparative Distribution of Under and Assistant Secretaries' Ages at Appointment, 1798–1938 and 1933–1965* [a]

	Age at Appointment [b]					
Source	*30's or Under*	*40's*	*50's*	*60's and Over*	Median Age [c]	Number of Persons
Macmahon and Millett [d] (1798-1938)	*24%*	*46%*	*24%*	*5%*	45	466
Present study (1933-1965)	*15*	*44*	*29*	*11*	47	628

[a] Percentages may not add to 100 because of rounding.

[b] The intervals are not precisely comparable. The intervals used here are those for the present study. Those used by Macmahon and Millett are: under 30 and 30-40 (combined), 40-50, 50-60, and over 60.

[c] Grouped median.

[d] Arthur W. Macmahon and John D. Millett, *Federal Administrators* (Columbia University Press, 1939), pp. 297-99.

Compared with other executives, the regulatory commissioners were in the middle of the group by age. They were a little *younger* than the commissioners studied by Herring, as Table 2.7 shows. The figures in the present study are very close to those computed by Bernstein for four of the commissions. This trend toward younger commissioners was shown in the case of the two commissions which could be compared directly—Interstate Commerce and Federal Trade.[21] The ICC median age was 51 for Herring's commissioners, 48 for those in the present study. The Federal Trade commissioners were closer: 50.5 for the Herring group, 49.5 for those studied here. Such a trend may be accounted for by Bernstein's discovery that

[21] There were too few cases to make comparisons worthwhile for other commissions.

TABLE 2.7.   *Distribution of Commissioners' Ages at Time of Appointment, Herring Study and Present Study*

Source	Age at Appointment				Median Age	Number of Persons
	30's and Under	*40's*	*50's*	*60's and Over*		
Herring study (1887-1936) [a]	*8%*	*32%*	*39%*	*21%*	49.5	130
Present study (1933-1965)	*18*	*41*	*29*	*12*	48	204
Bernstein study (from establishment of commissions to 1948) [b]	*20*	*38*	*29*	*14*	"47-48"	. . .

[a] Computed from Herring, *Federal Commissioners*, pp. 129-32.

[b] Marver H. Bernstein, *Regulating Business by Independent Commission* (Princeton University Press, 1955), p. 105. The study covers only FCC, FTC, NLRB, and SEC.

"there is some tendency to appoint younger men to relatively new commissions."[22]

For the other position levels, no detailed analysis was completed of age differentials by agency. Early work on this study showed that such differentials were small.

[22] Bernstein, *Regulating Business*, p. 105. Supporting figures are cited for NLRB, FTC, and SEC.

3

Occupational Backgrounds

THE FEDERAL POLITICAL EXECUTIVES included in the study came from a wide variety of occupations. Many had sufficient experience in two careers to justify listing them under both a principal occupation and a secondary calling. Of the whole group the bulk had been either public servants, lawyers, or businessmen. The largest group, 36 percent, had established careers in the public service, including 22 percent in federal jobs, either civil service or political. The practice of law was the primary occupation of another 26 percent, and 24 percent had been mainly in business. Many changed positions and even occupations before they became federal political executives, and it was sometimes difficult to classify them. Nevertheless, the patterns are clear and impressive, as shown in Chart 3.1 and Appendix Table E.1.[1]

Analyzed by administration, the patterns show some differences and similarities that confirm popular impressions. In President Eisen-

---

[1] See definitions of "principal occupation" and "secondary occupation" in Appendix B. In interpreting the tabulations and discussion in this chapter the reader should keep in mind that a political executive's principal occupation before appointment may change, because it is classified on the basis of duration and proximity to the type of political executive service being tabulated. Suppose, for example, that a man works three years as a practicing attorney, then serves six years as Assistant Secretary of Commerce, then becomes Secretary of Commerce. In assistant secretary tabulations his principal occupation is counted as law, and he has no secondary occupation. In cabinet secretary tabulations, his principal occupation is government service and his secondary occupation, law.

CHART 3.1. *Principal Occupations Before Appointment, by Adminis-tration*

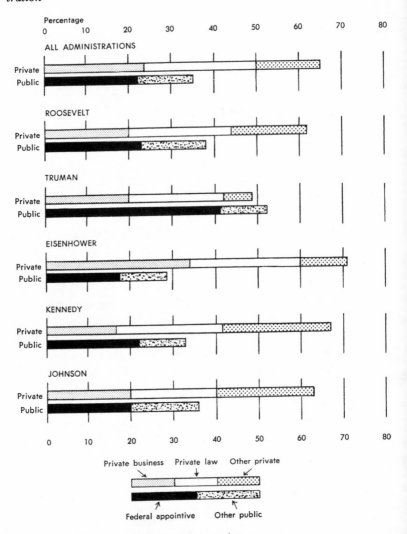

Note: Percentages may not add to 100 because of rounding.

hower's "businessmen's administration," the largest number were in fact industrial and commercial executives, such as General Motors president Charles E. Wilson, who became Secretary of Defense. President Truman, serving eight years himself after twelve years of the New Deal, was the largest user of public servants; Postmaster General Jesse Donaldson and Budget Director Frederick J. Lawton were two of the careerists whom he elevated. The proportion of lawyers did not vary much from one presidency to another. Educators were used far more by President Roosevelt (recall the criticisms of Rexford Tugwell and other New Deal professors) and by Presidents Kennedy and Johnson.

More than half of the group (58 percent) had identifiable second careers. The main picture does not change: public servants, lawyers, and businessmen head the list. Those with a primary career in one of these three areas generally had a secondary occupation in one of the other two. The patterns are rather similar for all five administrations, although executives whose secondary occupations had been in business were most numerous in the Eisenhower administration. (See Appendix Table E.2 for details.)

These occupational patterns for political executives are not very different from those for senators and congressmen. On Capitol Hill the major occupations are public service, law, business, agriculture, and teaching—in that order.[2]

If federal political executives are compared with big business executives, the figures show that the government is more likely to use lawyers and much less likely to choose scientists or engineers. Among the federal executives the lawyers comprised 26 percent, as compared with 12 percent of big business executives in 1950 and 11 percent in 1964. Scientists or engineers, however, numbered only 2 percent of the federal executives, while they came to 19 percent of the big business executives in 1950 and 35 percent in 1964.[3]

Occupational Patterns by Positions and Agencies

Executives' occupational histories vary a great deal from one position level to another, as shown in Table 3.1. Businessmen are the dominant group in all positions except assistant secretaries, general

[2] See the annual *Congressional Quarterly Almanacs* for figures. Close comparison of percentages is not possible because the present study counts only one principal occupation at a time for each person while the *Almanacs* count more than one for some senators and congressmen.

[3] *The Big Business Executive/1964* (Scientific American, 1965), p. 46.

TABLE 3.1. *Principal Occupations Before Appointment, by Position Level* [a]

					Position Level [b]					
Occupation	All Levels	Cabinet Secretary	Military Secretary	Under Secretary	Assistant Secretary	General Counsel	Administrator	Deputy Administrator	All Levels Except Commissioner	Commissioner
Business	24%	40%	56%	42%	26%	—	35%	29%	28%	12%
Law	26	23	30	24	24	57%	16	10	25	28
Education	7	2	4	6	9	7	10	2	7	4
Science or engineering	2	—	—	2	2	—	—	4	2	1
Other private	6	4	4	3	7	1	9	13	7	2
Total private	64	69	96	78	68	65	70	58	69	47
Public service elective	4	11	—	1	1	1	8	—	3	10
Appointive federal	22	11	—	16	25	25	16	32	22	23
Appointive nonfederal	9	10	4	5	5	8	6	10	6	20
Total government	36	31	4	22	32	35	30	42	31	53
Number of persons [c]	1,032	84	23	149	488	83	80	98	842	208

a Percentages may not add to subtotals or 100 because of rounding.

b Occupation before first appointment, regardless of the position level, is tabulated in the total for all positions. Occupation before the first noncommission appointment is tabulated for the "all levels except commissioner" column. Occupation before the first appointment at that position level is tabulated for breaks by position level.

c Numbers of persons in individual position levels do not add to the total for all position levels, because a person is counted once in each position level in which he served, but only once in the total for all position levels.

counsel, deputy administrators, and commissioners. Executives with a public service background are most numerous among the general counsel, deputy administrators, and especially the commissioners. The military department secretaries are overwhelmingly from the worlds of private business and law, and only a few have a background in public service. Lawyers are strongly represented at all levels except among the agency administrators and deputy administrators.

Commissioners

The regulatory commissioners have an occupational pattern of their own, as contrasted with the other executives. More of the commissioners have a background in public service than any other group. They are also the executives most likely to have worked in other levels of government, and they are exceeded only by the cabinet officers in the percentage who have held elective office. Comparatively few commissioners (12 percent) were businessmen. This pattern differs from that of the commissioners studied by Herring in one important respect: A far larger proportion of the commissioners in the present study had their principal occupations in public service, as shown in the following table.

SOURCE	BUSINESS	LAW	EDUCA-TION	SCIENCE OR ENGI-NEERING	OTHER PRIVATE	TOTAL PRIVATE	PUBLIC SERVICE
Herring study[4] (1887-1936)	17%	27%	10%	1%	10%	66%	34%
Present study (1933-1965)	12	28	4	1	2	47	53

The numbers of commissioners drawn from business, education, and other private pursuits (other than law) were correspondingly less.

Agency Patterns

Agency by agency, there are differences in the executives' prior careers, generally predictable in terms of the agencies' work (Ap-

---

[4] E. Pendleton Herring, *Federal Commissioners* (Harvard University Press, 1936), p. 114. Again, note that Herring studied a somewhat different complex of commissions.

pendix Table E.3). Businessmen were abundant in Navy (60 percent), Commerce (57 percent), Treasury (44 percent), Army (40 percent), Defense (39 percent), and Post Office and Air Force (each 34 percent). The largest proportions of educators were in the Departments of Agriculture (19 percent) and Health, Education, and Welfare (18 percent). Lawyers were everywhere but seemed relatively underrepresented in State and Agriculture—only 10 percent each. As for public servants, their prevalence in the commissions has already been mentioned. The Department of State, rotating foreign service officers through assistant secretaryships, was the largest user (51 percent) of federal employees. Justice, Post Office, Interior, Agriculture, and HEW also promoted substantial numbers: from 19 to 24 percent of their executives had federal appointive posts as their principal prior occupations. Army (2 percent) and Navy (7 percent) were least likely to appoint from within the federal service.[5]

Many appointments seemed particularly apt, considering the executives' particular interests. Marion Folsom as a business executive had pioneered in social insurance matters long before he became HEW Secretary. Robert Murphy was a career "diplomat among warriors" before his emphasis upon a politico-military approach to foreign affairs helped elevate him to Deputy Under Secretary and then Under Secretary of State. Stewart Udall was a practicing outdoorsman and reclamation-minded congressman before he became Secretary of the Interior.

Business: Type, Size, Relevance

Among the executives who had been businessmen, the largest category (44 percent) had been in manufacturing companies. Ranking second were financial institutions, with 23 percent. Small fractions came from other segments of private industry: trade, public utilities, mining, construction, agriculture, and others.

The types of businesses from which executives were recruited did

---

[5] Many officials with federal service as their principal occupation before political executive appointment were not career officials in a formal sense but (like Oscar Chapman and Frank Pace) had served for years in other noncareer positions.

not vary appreciably from one presidency to another, with two exceptions: Presidents Kennedy and Johnson appointed fewer executives (30 and 27 percent, respectively) from manufacturing industries and correspondingly more from "other" industries (Table 3.2).

TABLE 3.2. *Types of Business Engaged in by Federal Political Executives Whose Principal Occupation Before Appointment Was Business, by Administration* [a]

Type of Business	Administration [b]					
	All Five	Roose-velt	Truman	Eisen-hower	Ken-nedy	Johnson
Manufacturing	44%	43%	44%	45%	30%	27%
Finance	23	27	24	27	21	23
Trade	8	4	3	11	9	10
Transportation, communication, utilities	8	8	10	5	6	7
Mining	5	8	5	2	9	3
Construction	1	—	—	1	3	3
Other	11	10	14	10	21	27
Number of persons [c]	240	49	63	112	33	30

[a] Percentages may not add to 100 because of rounding.

[b] Occupation before the first political executive position, regardless of the administration, is tabulated in the total of all persons. Occupation before the first appointment (or reappointment) in that administration is tabulated in the breakdown by administration.

[c] Numbers of persons in individual administrations do not add to the total for all administrations, because a person is counted once in each administration he served, but only once in the total for all five administrations. He is dropped from the count if his principal occupation before appointment shifts to a field other than business.

Size of Business

The widespread impression that more federal political executives come from large businesses than from small ones is correct. But the equally widespread impression that Eisenhower was the President who appointed the largest proportion of persons from large business is incorrect: President Kennedy chose the largest proportion, followed in order by Johnson, Truman, Eisenhower, and Roosevelt. President Eisenhower did, however, appoint the largest number of executives from both large and small businesses (Table 3.3.).

TABLE 3.3. *Appointments of Federal Political Executives from Large or Small Businesses, by Administration*

Size of Business or Financial Institution	Administration [a]					
	All Five	Roose-velt	Truman	Eisen-hower	Ken-nedy	Johnson
Largest 500 [b]	56%	44%	60%	56%	65%	61%
Smaller firms	44	56	40	44	35	39
Number of persons [c]	199	39	43	99	26	23

[a] Occupation before the first political executive position, regardless of the administration, is tabulated in the total of all persons. Occupation before the first appointment (or reappointment) in that administration is tabulated in the breakdown by administration.

[b] Large businesses are those included in the *Fortune* Directory of the 500 Largest U.S. Industrial Corporations. (Sales figures are the criteria of size.) Large financial institutions are those included in the list of the largest investment firms supplied by the Investment Bankers Association of America.

[c] Numbers of persons in individual administrations do not add to the total for all administrations, because a person is counted once in each administration he served, but only once in the total for all five administrations.

Large Defense Contractors

Since World War II, questions have been raised about the relationships between large defense contractors and the agencies with which they do business. President Eisenhower in his farewell address drew renewed attention to these relationships. To explore one aspect of this general question, a special analysis was made to see how many political executives came to the government from employment by large defense contractors.[6] The executives included were those who had worked for a major defense contractor within two years before appointment to a political executive position, or to another federal position which immediately preceded appointment to the executive position.

The results show that 4 percent of the executives appointed from 1945 through 1965 had been so employed. Departments and agencies dealing with defense matters were of course the largest users of such persons. Analyzed by administration, the figures show clearly

---

[6] The 100 largest defense contractors, as listed by the Department of Defense. See Appendix B for a more detailed definition.

larger percentages of contractor alumni in the Kennedy and Johnson administrations than in the Truman and Eisenhower administrations. (However, Presidents Kennedy and Johnson made fewer executive appointments than their predecessors.)

Whether the proportions are too low or too high is a question beyond this study. Other commentators may consider whether the figures more frequently represent potential conflicts of interest or a wise use of skilled people, and whether the rising trend is alarming or gratifying. The figures appear in more detail in Table 3.4. The percentages should be interpreted thus: Of the executives appointed by President Truman to defense-related agencies, 10 percent had been employed by major defense contractors within two years before their executive appointments or other federal government appointments preceding them. Of those he appointed to other agencies, only 1 percent had been so employed.

TABLE 3.4. *Federal Political Executives Formerly Employed by Major Defense Contractors,*[a] *by Administration and Agency Category*

Administration	All Agencies	Defense-Related Agencies [b]	Other Agencies [c]	Number of Persons [d]
Four administrations	4%	12%	1%	710
Truman	3	10	1	254
Eisenhower	4	13	1	290
Kennedy	6	20	—	162
Johnson [e]	4	17 [e]	—	135

[a] Principal occupation before government service, or occupation immediately before government service, was as employee of a large defense contractor.

[b] Each person is counted once under "Four administrations" and once under each President for whom he served as a federal political executive in any of the following agencies: Defense, Army, Navy, Air Force, Office of Civil and Defense Mobilization, Office of Defense Mobilization, Office of War Mobilization, Office of War Mobilization and Reconversion, War Production Board, Federal Civil Defense Administration, Economic Stabilization Agency, Defense Production Administration, and Office of Emergency Planning. If a person held appointments in both "Defense-Related" and "Other" agencies, he is included in the former.

[c] Each person is counted once under "Four administrations" and once under each President he served, excluding those counted in "Defense-Related Agencies" and the commissioners.

[d] Numbers of persons in individual administrations do not add to the total for all administrations, because a person is counted once in each administration he served, but only once in the total for all four administrations.

[e] All appointments credited to President Johnson were of persons who continued in his administration for more than six months, having originally been appointed by President Kennedy; they were, therefore, counted as reappointments.

Regulated Industries

A related question studied was the extent to which regulatory commissioners had been employed in, or retained by, the industries or functions which they were now to regulate.[7] For the four commissions working with a clear-cut segment of industry it is easy to determine whether a person was employed in the industry regulated: these are the Civil Aeronautics Board, the Federal Communications Commission, the Federal Power Commission, and the Interstate Commerce Commission. The other three, the Federal Trade Commission, the National Labor Relations Board, and the Securities and Exchange Commission, have such pervasive functions that it was more difficult to decide which commissioners had been employed in a field of direct concern to that commission. Thus there is a need for case-by-case analysis before confident generalizations can be made.

The study showed, granting this difficulty, a wide variation among the commissions. In the clear-cut group, appointments from the industries concerned were more frequent in the ICC (21 percent) and CAB (19 percent), clearly lower in the FCC (14 percent) and FPC (12 percent). Among the other three commissions, only one member of the FTC and two of the NLRB seemed to acquire jurisdiction over functions in which they had worked. One out of every three SEC commissioners clearly had a background in corporate finance. The detailed figures (Appendix Table E.4) show that President Truman selected 28 percent of his commissioners from regulated industries or functions; President Eisenhower, 20 percent; President Kennedy, 12 percent; and President Roosevelt, 11 percent. President Johnson's percentage was 29, but this represents only two appointments, both to the SEC.

Such appointments may be interpreted as intelligent selection of qualified candidates or as quiet surrender to a dangerous cabal; either view is oversimplified. Commissioners vary extensively in their

---

[7] Attorneys whose practice was primarily concerned with such industries or functions were included, along with persons directly employed. Commissioners included were those employed in or retained by such an industry or function within two years before appointment as commissioner or to another federal position which immediately preceded the commissioner position.

qualifications and motivations, and every appointment is the result of many different factors.

Previous Public Service

Any impression that federal political executives are neophytes in public service is clearly refuted by the figures presented here and in Chapter 4. Public service, as noted earlier, was the principal prior occupation of 36 percent of the political executives and the secondary occupation of 22 percent. Some form of government work was at least a part-time concern of a large majority of appointees. The analysis turns now to the nature of this public service and its duration.

Types of Federal Service

Before their appointments as federal political executives, these officials had done many different types of federal work. The predominant categories were full-time jobs in the executive branch, primarily in lower noncareer jobs (Appendix Table E.5). Many had served in more than one type of federal assignment.

For every 100 appointments to federal political executive positions:[8]

37 of the men chosen for such appointments had served in noncareer jobs (such as legislative aides or "assistants to . . .") in other agencies than the one in which they were then serving as political executives;

24 had held noncareer jobs in the same agencies, that is, those in which they were appointed as political executives;

14 had career jobs in the same agencies;[9]

[8] The discussion here and in the three subsections following is in terms of the 1,567 appointments rather than the 1,041 federal political executives. It was pointed out in Chap. 1 that many executives had more than one appointment. Each time the President makes an appointment, his selection may be a person who has had one or more previous appointments, either as an executive or in some other post.

[9] Such career jobs were not all in the competitive civil service or other federal merit systems. If a person spent over five years in an exempt position, this was counted as a career job.

11 had career jobs in other agencies;

29 had held other political executive posts in the same agency;

8 had been political executives in other agencies;

3 had been commissioners in other agencies;

6 had served in Congress;

1 had been in the federal judiciary;

7 had held political party office at the national level;[10]

18 had had part-time federal assignments, most of them in combination with other federal service;

and only 15 had no federal service of any kind.

Presidents Kennedy and Truman selected the highest percentages of executives who had been career employees. President Roosevelt, partly because of the New Deal's massive need for fresh talent, chose the lowest percentage of careerists. President Johnson's retention of many New Frontier executives gave him the highest percentage of appointees who had been political executives in the same agency. President Kennedy chose the largest proportion who had been political party officers. Otherwise, differences among the administrations were not significant.

DIFFERENCES AMONG POSITION LEVELS. There was a strong tendency to appoint persons who had served in other political executive positions (Appendix Table E.6). Many of these were promotions or transfers. Cyrus Vance, for example, moved from General Counsel of Defense to Secretary of the Army to Deputy Secretary of Defense; David Bell went from Director of the Bureau of the Budget to Administrator of the Agency for International Development. Other examples at various position levels follow.

At the cabinet officer level, 40 percent of appointments were of political executives who had served in the same department (Under Secretary of State Dean Acheson became Secretary); 29 percent were of political executives who had served in other departments and agencies (Marion B. Folsom moved from Under Secretary of the Treasury to Secretary of Health, Education, and Welfare).

---

[10] National committeeman, or some other high post. Strictly speaking, this work is not federal service, but has much in common with noncareer federal positions of professional and administrative types.

The figures were even higher for the military secretaries: 50 percent had been political executives in the same military department (Air Force Secretary Zuckert had served in an earlier administration as Assistant Secretary); 29 percent elsewhere in the Department of Defense (Wilber Brucker was General Counsel of Defense before he was Secretary of the Army); and 8 percent had been political executives in other agencies (President Truman appointed Budget Director Frank Pace to be Secretary of the Army).

Large majorities of assistant secretary and general counsel appointees had been noncareer employees, either of the same agency, or of others (Assistant Secretary of the Interior Dale E. Doty had been Assistant to the Secretary). The political executive positions most frequently filled from career ranks were deputy agency administrators with assistant secretaries next (Deputy Administrator—and later Administrator—of the Veterans Administration William J. Driver had been a career VA employee; Assistant Secretary of the Navy Graeme Bannerman was a career employee of the Office of the Secretary of Defense).

The political executive positions most often filled by former senators and congressmen were cabinet secretaryships; 16 percent of the appointees had served on the Hill (Senator Cordell Hull became Secretary of State). Eleven percent of the commissioners had served in the Senate or House (Civil Aeronautics Board member Chan Gurney was a former senator).

DIFFERENCES BY AGENCY. When political executives' previous federal experience is analyzed by agency, there are variations which result both from the political relationships of the various agencies and from their executive personnel practices. Former legislators were most likely to be found in the Federal Trade Commission, the Civil Aeronautics Board, the Department of the Interior, the National Labor Relations Board, and the Department of Health, Education, and Welfare. Former political party officers had an affinity for Post Office and HEW. The Department of State, with its promotion and transfer practices, frequently appointed careerists from within. The commissions, military departments, Interior, State, and Justice took large proportions of their appointees from among political executives who had already served in those departments. (Complete percentages appear in Appendix Table E.7.)

COMMISSIONERS. Among the regulatory commissions, 85 percent of the men selected for appointment had had some federal experience, as contrasted with 72 percent of the commissioners studied by Herring.[11] Another comparison shows that 13 percent of Herring's commissioners had served in Congress,[12] compared with 11 percent of the commissioner appointees in the present study. Other comparisons with Herring's work in this respect are uninformative because of differences between the two studies in methodology and coverage.

There are a few significant differences among the commissions covered in the present study (Appendix Table E.7). Only in the Federal Communications Commission and the Securities and Exchange Commission were career staff members promoted to commissionerships in significant proportions (22 and 21 percent of appointees, respectively).[13] FCC was also the commission making the greatest use of careerists from other agencies (28 percent), followed by the Federal Trade Commission (18 percent). As already reported, ex-congressmen were used most in the Federal Trade Commission and the Civil Aeronautics Board, with the National Labor Relations Board third. Noncareer employees from other agencies were used heavily in all commissions (39 percent of appointees), particularly in CAB (56 percent). As for noncareer employees who became commissioners in their own agencies, this occurred significantly only in NLRB (20 percent of board appointees).

Length of Federal Administrative Service

It has been established that a large majority of federal political executives served previously in full-time federal positions, career or noncareer. How long did they serve? Special tabulations were

---

[11] Herring, *Federal Commissioners*, p. 126.
[12] *Ibid.*, p. 51.
[13] One former career employee, Manuel Cohen, is SEC Chairman at this writing.

made of length of federal administrative service to answer this question.[14]

The 643 political executives who had federal administrative service (63 percent of the total number of persons studied) had a median of 5.2 years of such service (Table 3.5). About 30 percent of these 643 had served over 10 years. Executives with no federal administrative service were most frequently found in the Eisenhower administration. The people with longer service were distributed through the Truman, Kennedy, and Johnson administrations, with Kennedy appointees having the highest median service. There was a concentration in the Kennedy and Johnson administrations of officials with more than 15 years of federal administrative service —suggesting that a group of veteran federal employees whose service began during or before World War II had been recognized with political executive appointments.

TABLE 3.5. *Distribution of Years of Federal Administrative Service Before Appointment, by Administration* [a]

Administration [b]	No Service	Years of Service					Median of Those with Service [c]	Number of Persons [d]
		1-2	3-5	6-10	11-15	16 and Over		
All five	37%	18%	14%	11%	7%	11%	5.2	1,027
Roosevelt	32	22	14	17	3	12	5.0	268
Truman	21	13	17	16	19	13	8.3	315
Eisenhower	44	15	15	10	4	11	4.9	346
Kennedy	30	21	10	10	9	18	9.3	191
Johnson	8	12	36	15	11	18	5.3	146

[a] Percentages may not add to 100 because of rounding.

[b] The figures for all five administrations include service before the first appointment, regardless of administration. Breaks by administration include service before the first appointment in that administration.

[c] Grouped median.

[d] Numbers of persons in individual administrations do not add to the total for all administrations, because a person is counted once in each administration he served, but only once in the total for all five administrations.

[14] Federal administrative service was defined to include time served in (1) political executive positions, (2) full-time administrative positions in the executive, legislative, and judicial branches of the federal government, and (3) professional military service. It does not include service as a legislator or judge, or nonprofessional military or part-time service.

Looking at the location of this earlier service, one finds that 35 percent of all executives studied had prior federal administrative service in the same agency;[15] and 43 percent had such service in other agencies. The median period of such service in the same agency was 4.3 years, and in other agencies 4.1 years. Presidents Truman and Johnson appointed the highest percentages of persons whose service had been in the same agency. These two, plus President Kennedy, chose the highest proportions of executives who had administrative service in other agencies (Appendix Table E.8).

Of the various executive position levels studied, the military secretaries were most likely to have had federal administrative service—nine out of ten—but they had the lowest median period of service (Table 3.6). Over three out of four of the under secretaries and deputy administrators were credited with federal administrative ser-

TABLE 3.6. *Percentages and Median Years of Service of Federal Political Executives with Prior Federal Administrative Service, by Position Level* [a]

Position Level [b]	Percentage with Federal Administrative Service	Median Years [c]	Number of Persons [d]
All levels	*63%*	5.2	1,027
Cabinet secretary	*63*	6.4	84
Military secretary	*91*	3.3	23
Under secretary	*78*	4.3	149
Assistant secretary	*69*	5.1	486
General counsel	*68*	5.2	83
Administrator	*62*	5.5	80
Deputy administrator	*78*	7.0	98
Commissioner	*57*	6.6	205

a For a detailed distribution, see Appendix Table E.10.

b The figures for all levels include service before the first appointment, regardless of the position level to which appointed. Breaks by position level include service before the first appointment to that position level.

c Grouped medians.

d Numbers of persons in individual position levels do not add to the total for all position levels, because a person is counted once in each position level in which he served, but only once in the total for all position levels.

15 The agency where first appointed as a federal political executive.

vice, many of them having been promoted from other positions. The commissioners had the lowest percentage of persons with such service, but relatively high median service. (See Appendix Table E.9 for details.)

Nonfederal Service

Experience in other levels of government was less prevalent than federal experience but still significant. Three out of every eight federal political executives had held positions in state, local, or international public service, or had been officers of state or local political organizations. Some had been state governors, state legislators, or local elected officials, as Appendix Table E.10 shows. Many more had held state or local appointive office. In general, a higher proportion of the regulatory commissioners than of the other executives had had state or local experience.

The backgrounds of these commissioners reveal both similarities and contrasts with the commissioners studied by Herring. The contrasts are impressive, but hard to interpret: much larger proportions of the earlier group had had nonfederal public service (76 percent, compared with 45 percent). Far more of the Herring group had been mayors, councilmen, or other local elected officials—24 percent, compared with 9 percent of the commissioners in the present study. Herring also found more state legislators: 15 percent, as against 9 percent here. As to similarities, former state governors made up 2 percent of each group, and the proportion of state and local judges was also close—9 percent in the 1936 study, 7 percent in the present study.[16] "The states," said Herring, "provide one training ground from which some notable administrators have come."[17] He went on to give favorable attention to service on state regulatory bodies corresponding to those federal commissions to which the men were later appointed. State railroad agencies and the Interstate Commerce Commission were singled out particularly to make his point.

A special tabulation made as part of the present study shows that a significant number of Federal Power commissioners during the past thirty years had experience on state utility commissions: of

[16] Herring, *Federal Commissioners*, pp. 45, 124.
[17] *Ibid.*, p. 46.

those initially appointed to the FPC by the five most recent Presidents, 43 percent had held high positions in state power agencies. When the whole group of commissioners is examined, 13 percent of those in the Herring study had been state public utility commissioners,[18] and 13 percent of those in the present study had served in state counterpart agencies (Table 3.7).

TABLE 3.7. *Commissioners Who Held High Positions in Counterpart State Regulatory Agencies Before Appointment to Federal Commissions*

Commission	Members Who Served in State Counterpart Agencies [a]	Total Number of Persons
All seven	*13%*	203
Civil Aeronautics Board	*11*	27
Federal Communications Commission	*9*	35
Federal Power Commission	*43*	23
Federal Trade Commission	—	24
Interstate Commerce Commission	*21*	28
National Labor Relations Board	*8*	25
Securities and Exchange Commission	*7*	41

a Some commissioners had held high positions in state agencies which were not counterparts of the federal commissions to which they were later appointed. Their service in such noncounterpart agencies is counted among "other" state officials in Appendix Table E.10.

Total Length of Government Administrative Service, Federal and Nonfederal

To reemphasize a well-established fact, the federal political executives as a group are experienced public servants. Putting together all the types of prior federal and nonfederal administrative experience accumulated by them, three out of four (73 percent) had such experience. The median duration was about six years, one year longer than median federal administrative service.

Commissioners were more likely than other federal political executives to have had government administrative experience—and for longer periods: 78 percent of them had such experience, with a

18 *Ibid.*, p. 24.

median of 7.4 years. Of other federal political executives, 72 percent had such experience, with a median of 5.5 years. Truman and Kennedy appointees had the longest periods of prior government administrative service, and Eisenhower appointees were lowest. Commissioners appointed by Truman and Kennedy were particularly high in total government administrative service. (See Chart 3.2 for a graphic comparison by administration and Appendix Table E.11 for detailed figures.)

CHART 3.2. *Median Years of Total Government Administrative Service Before Appointment, by Administration*

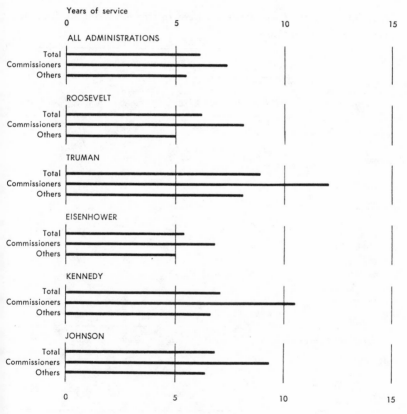

Note: Medians are only for those having service.

Positions Held Just Before Appointment

As the discussion turns from occupational backgrounds to jobs immediately preceding executive appointment, the pattern of previous federal service remains strong. Seven out of every ten appointees were in government positions just before their federal political executive appointments. Three out of ten went from one political executive appointment to another. Another three out of ten came from other federal appointments.

The pattern of positions immediately before appointment (Table 3.8) is almost the opposite of principal occupations (Chart 3.1 and Appendix Table E.1). That is, a heavy majority of the executives

TABLE 3.8. *Categories of Positions Held Immediately Before Appointment, by Administration* [a]

| Category of Position | Administration | | | | | |
	All Five	*Roosevelt*	*Truman*	*Eisen-hower*	*Kennedy*	*Johnson*
Business	*13%*	*9%*	*10%*	*20%*	*15%*	*3%*
Law	*11*	*11*	*10*	*14*	*15*	*3*
Other private	*6*	*7*	*3*	*6*	*17*	*1*
Total private	*30*	*26*	*23*	*41*	*47*	*7*
Federal political executives (including commissioners)	*32*	*27*	*36*	*24*	*18*	*75*
Other federal non-career appointive	*22*	*29*	*26*	*20*	*17*	*13*
Federal career	*7*	*6*	*10*	*6*	*8*	*3*
Elective (federal, state, or local)	*4*	*4*	*3*	*4*	*5*	—
Other	*5*	*6*	*3*	*5*	*6*	*3*
Total government	*69*	*74*	*76*	*59*	*53*	*93*
Retired	*0.2*	—	*0.5*	*0.2*	—	—
Number of appointments	1,556	355	400	433	212	156

[a] Percentages may not add to subtotals or 100 because of rounding.

had their principal occupations in the private sector, but a heavy majority of positions immediately prior were in the public service.

Presidents Kennedy and Eisenhower made the highest percentages of appointments directly from private life, 47 and 41 percent. Both were making a fresh start after years of government by the opposite political party and could have been expected to appoint men from outside the government. President Roosevelt's lower percentage (26) of appointees from private jobs can be accounted for by: (1) the huge expansion of the federal government during his long administration, leading him to upgrade and transfer many of his appointees; and (b) the lack of rapport between him and the business community.

President Johnson's extremely high percentage (75) of appointments from other political executive positions are mainly carry-overs from the Kennedy administration. President Truman, whose confidence in public servants was demonstrated by figures cited earlier, made the highest proportion of appointments from federal career positions (10 percent). President Eisenhower was the leader in the businessman category in this analysis, as in others.

All five Presidents made relatively few appointments directly from the federal career service—a mean of 7 percent—apparently preferring to transfer or promote political executives or to promote other noncareer employees. Yet some former career employees moved into a succession of political executive positions or other noncareer positions. Roger W. Jones, for example, went from a career job in the Bureau of the Budget to Deputy Director of the Bureau, then was Chairman of the Civil Service Commission, then Deputy Under Secretary of State.

The idea is sometimes advanced that Presidents are more likely to make political executive appointments from within the federal service late in their administrations. At the beginning they tend to appoint from outside ("fresh start," "new blood," "reward those who helped in the campaign," and so on). As times goes on, two changes occur: (1) the administration, no longer new, loses some of its appeal to outsiders; and (2) the chief executive gains confidence in federal employees, both career and noncareer.

A special tabulation was made to test this line of thought. Counts were made at various dates of political executives whose jobs immediately prior to their executive appointments had been in federal service. The results appear in Chart 3.3. In each administration except President Truman's the percentage of executives appointed from inside the government rises, thus supporting the hypothesis. Several explanations can be offered of the opposite trend in the Truman administration (which is a relatively small decline): (1) President Truman started high in the proportion of appointments from inside and may well have reached the limit which our political system will tolerate. Truman's low point, however, is nearly as high as Eisenhower's high point. (2) The end was in sight for his presidency, so federal employees may have been reluctant to accept such

CHART 3.3. *Proportions of Federal Political Executives Who Were in Federal Service Immediately Before Appointment, Selected Dates, 1936–65*

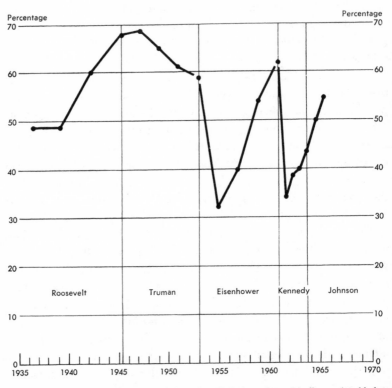

Note: Chart covers 1,048 federal political executives, 7 of whom were originally appointed before the Roosevelt administration.

vulnerable posts. (3) The sudden beginning of the Korean conflict in 1950 may have resulted in an influx of outsiders to help with the defense effort—although World War II apparently did not have this effect in the Roosevelt administration.

Analysis by Position Level

When the executives' prior jobs are analyzed by position level (Appendix Table E.12), concentrations of businessmen are found at all levels except general counsel and commissioners. Lawyers are also sprinkled throughout except for administrators and deputy administrators. Commissioners were less likely to be appointed from jobs in private life than were other federal political executives—21 percent, as compared with 33 percent.

Turning to the public service as a source of appointees, one finds that promotion or reappointment of political executives was used to fill a large proportion of positions as cabinet officer and commissioner (44 percent), under secretary (48 percent), and military department head (62 percent). Noncareer employees were frequently promoted to become assistant secretaries, general counsel, or deputy administrators. The positions most frequently filled directly from federal career ranks were deputy administrators (14 percent), assistant secretaries (9 percent), commissioners (8 percent), and general counsel (6 percent).

The positions to which the highest proportion of appointments was made from the public service as a whole were deputy administrators and commissioners, with reappointments accounting in large measure for the high commissioner figure.

4

Tenure

HOW LONG DID THESE federal political executives serve? The question of tenure is crucial. Relatively short service by political executives (in comparison with the tenure of career officials) is expected in a responsive democracy. If the President is to have effective control, he must be able to replace cabinet and subcabinet officers as he wishes, particularly when there is a transition from one political party to another.[1] Executives may also move in and out of political posts for purposes of career mobility—so that their experience can be used to best advantage and so that able persons may move between government and industry or government and education. Many executives have come into federal service with only short-term commitments.[2]

On the other hand, short tenure has obvious disadvantages. An executive of even superior ability takes perhaps a year or more on the job to become fully productive, learning the issues, programs, systems, technical problems, and personalities involved in his work.[3] Unless he has been promoted or transferred from another high federal job—and a relevant one—he finds that his previous experience

[1] See discussions in Laurin Henry, *Presidential Transitions* (Brookings Institution, 1960); Paul T. David (ed.), *The Presidential Election and Transition, 1960–61* (Brookings Institution, 1961); and David T. Stanley, *Changing Administrations* (Brookings Institution, 1965).

[2] Marver H. Bernstein, *The Job of the Federal Executive* (Brookings Institution, 1958), pp. 162–63.

[3] Dean E. Mann with Jameson W. Doig, *The Assistant Secretaries: Problems and Processes of Appointment* (Brookings Institution, 1965), pp. 6–7, 227, 230.

has done little to prepare him. The sooner he leaves the government, the more his painfully acquired job experience goes to waste.

The problem of executive tenure is neither new nor easy to solve. Both the second Hoover Commission in the mid-1950's and the Senate Subcommittee on National Policy Machinery in 1960 found the tenure of federal political executives to be deplorably short and offered some possible remedies.[4] Since then, executive salaries have been increased and intensive, well-organized recruiting programs have been used by Presidents Kennedy and Johnson.[5] These steps have improved the government's ability to replace political executives, but the basic problem of short tenure remains.

Concern with brief tenure in the national security field prompted the Senate, in 1960, to pass the following resolution recommended by its Subcommittee on National Policy Machinery:

> . . . that it is the sense of the Senate that individuals appointed to administrative and policymaking posts should be willing to serve for a period long enough to permit them to contribute effectively in their assigned tasks. . . .[6]

The problem can be overemphasized, however, by undue concentration upon position tenure figures—the length of time a person serves in one particular executive position. Both the Hoover Commission and the Senate Subcommittee contributed to this overemphasis. The problem is actually mitigated by two factors: (1) Many of the men studied here (63 percent) served for significant periods in other full-time federal jobs before they were appointed as political executives; and (2) 37 percent had more than one political ex-

[4] Commission on Organization of the Executive Branch of Government, *Personnel and Civil Service* (1955), pp. 25–36, and *Task Force Report on Personnel and Civil Service* (1955), pp. 1–47; *Resolution Expressing Concern of Senate over Turnover in Administrative and Policymaking Posts,* S. Rept. 1753, 86 Cong. 2 sess. (1960). See also John A. Perkins, "Staffing Democracy's Top Side," *Public Administration Review,* Vol. 17 (Winter 1957), pp. 1–9. See Table 4.2 below, p. 60, for tenure figures.

[5] See Stanley, *Changing Administrations,* p. 3; "Help Wanted," *Forbes,* Vol. 96 (July 15, 1965), pp. 32–33; and "How LBJ Picks His Men," *Nation's Business,* Vol. 53 (July 1965), pp. 36–37, 78, 80.

[6] S. Res. 338, *Congressional Record,* Vol. 106, Pt. 12, 86 Cong. 2 sess. (1960), p. 15705.

ecutive appointment. Thus their service to the government was longer than position tenure figures would indicate.[7]

What were the actual figures? How long did these executives stay in their jobs, in their agencies, in the government? They stayed two to three years. The median political executive worked in his position 28 months, in his agency 31 months, and in the federal government 37 months.[8]

These are certainly short periods of time, considering the scope of the executives' responsibilities. The reader should recall, however, that the median executive had two years of prior federal administrative service, plus his three years of government tenure as a political executive—five years of significant full-time federal experience. If one considers only the 63 percent with federal administrative experience, the median figure rises to a total of eight years. Thus the political executives have much more experience than mere executive tenure statistics or the statements of concerned critics would lead one to believe.

Differences Among Position Levels

Closer analysis, job by job, is needed, for it is apparent to casual newspaper readers, as well as to political analysts, that cabinet officers stay in office longer than assistant secretaries and under secretaries do. Members of the cabinet enjoy greater prestige, which may well encourage them to remain. They also have no higher job to move into, unlike assistant secretaries.

Median tenure figures by position level are given in Table 4.1. There are, of course, wide tenure variations within position levels. Frances Perkins served over 12 years as Secretary of Labor; Martin Durkin served 8 months. Wesley D'Ewart was Assistant Secretary of the Interior for 9 months; James Wakelin was Assistant Secretary of the Navy for nearly 5 years.

[7] See above, Chap. 3; also Chap. 1.
[8] All at the political executive level. See Appendix A for coverage and Appendix B for definitions of position, agency, and government tenure.

TABLE 4.1. *Median Tenure in Position and in Agency, by Position Level* [a]

Position Level	Median Position Tenure (Months)	Median Agency Tenure (Months)
All levels	28	31
All levels except Commissioner	25	28
All levels except Cabinet secretary and Commissioner	25	27
Cabinet secretary	40	40
Military secretary	25	25
Under secretary	21	22
Assistant secretary	26	30
General counsel	25	31
Administrator	26	26
Deputy administrator	19	23
Commissioner	54	55 [b]

[a] See explanations in Appendix A concerning coverage of tenure tables and computation of tenure and medians.

[b] Agency tenure differs from position tenure because two FCC members served in a predecessor agency, the Federal Radio Commission, and their service in the latter was counted in agency tenure but not in position tenure.

Except for cabinet officers and commissioners, the medians are all close to 2 years, both in the position level and in the agency. The long tenure of commissioners results from their being appointed for statutory terms of 5, 6, or 7 years. Even though many of them serve less than a full term, their expectations are for a longer period of service than most of the political executives.[9]

Periods of tenure for all executives ranged from 1 month to over 21 years, but there were variations among position levels in the way these periods were clustered (Chart 4.1 and Appendix Table F.1). Most of the military secretaries are bunched together in the 1-to-3 year brackets. Under secretaries, administrators, and deputy administrators are spread out further, and the others still more.

[9] Commissioners' patterns of appointments and tenure are analyzed below, p. 68.

CHART 4.1. *Distribution of Years of Position Tenure, by Position Level*

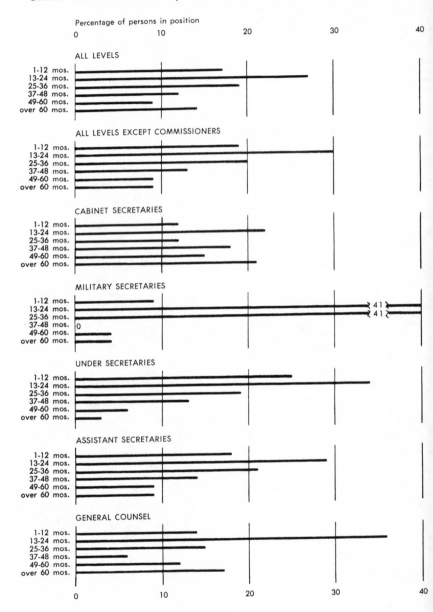

Note: Percentages may not add to 100 because of rounding. See Appendix Table F.1 for more detailed information.

Chart 4.1.   *Distribution of Years of Position Tenure, by Position Level*
(Continued)

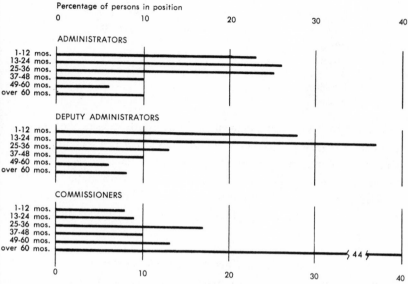

Cabinet officers and general counsel (and commissioners) are more
likely to have spent more than 5 years in their position levels. For
all the position levels except commissioners, the largest (modal)
group were those who spent from 1 to 2 years on the job.

To look in another way at the position tenure of all the executives
except commissioners:

1 out of 5 stayed in his position level no more than 1 year
1 out of 2 stayed over 2 years
1 out of 3 stayed over 3 years
1 out of 5 stayed over 4 years
1 out of 11 stayed over 5 years

Some Comparisons

The tenure of federal political executives is short when compared
with that of members of the cabinet of the mayor of New York City,
the second largest government in the United States, during approxi-

mately the same period (1933–1958), as may be seen in the table below.[10]

APPOINTING MAYOR	NUMBER OF APPOINTEES	AVERAGE TENURE (MONTHS)
O'Brien	47	57.5
LaGuardia	115	54.7
O'Dwyer	81	36.2
Impellitteri	51	51.4
Wagner	60	50.5

It is difficult to reach conclusions about trends in tenure of federal political executives. In view of the emphasis that the second Hoover Commission placed upon political executive tenure, an effort was made to compare the commission's averages with data from the present study.[11] The results, presented in Table 4.2, cannot be considered conclusive, except that tenure of department heads was

TABLE 4.2. *Comparison of Average (Mean) Position Tenure, Second Hoover Commission and Present Study, by Position Level*

Position Level	Second Hoover Commission Averages [a] (Months)		Present Study (Months)	
	1933-48	1948-52	1933-52 [b]	1953-60
Secretary [c]	49	42.5	42	40
Under secretary	23	23	22	27
Assistant secretary	32	28	32	32

a Commission on Organization . . . of the Government, *Personnel and Civil Service*, p. 26. Figures in these columns are difficult to interpret because of uncertainty about how periods of tenure beginning or ending in 1948 were classified. It was not feasible to split the Brookings study figures in 1948.

b The 1933-1952 break includes the total position tenure of all persons appointed or reappointed by Roosevelt or appointed by Truman. The 1953-1960 break includes the total position tenure of all persons appointed or reappointed by Eisenhower.

c Includes cabinet and military secretaries.

10 Theodore J. Lowi, *At the Pleasure of the Mayor* (Free Press of Glencoe, 1964), p. 131.

11 Averages (means) should not be strongly relied upon because these measures of central tendency are unduly influenced by comparatively few instances of very long tenure. For this reason, tenure figures are generally presented in this study in the form of medians and distributions.

longer in the early years (largely because of the long service of some of President Roosevelt's cabinet) and the tenure of under secretaries was longer in the later years. A clear-cut trend to shorter tenure appears when a comparison is made with Macmahon's and Millett's figures on under and assistant secretaries (Table 4.3).

TABLE 4.3. *Comparative Distribution of Position Tenure of Under and Assistant Secretaries, 1798–1938 and 1933–1965* [a]

Source	Position Tenure (Months)						Median (Months)	Number of Persons in Positions [b]
	0-12	13-24	25-36	37-48	49-60	61 and Over		
Macmahon and Millett (1798-1938) [c]	15%	22%	22%	18%	11%	14%	28	539
Present study (1933-1965)	20	31	20	14	8	7	24 [d]	589

Note: Percentages may not add to 100 because of rounding.
[a] Recall that assistant secretaries are far more numerous than under secretaries.
[b] See Appendix A for an explanation of differences in coverage between tables presenting position tenure only and those which compare position tenure with agency and government tenure.
[c] Arthur W. Macmahon and John D. Millett, *Federal Administrators* (Columbia University Press, 1939), pp. 296-99.
[d] Grouped median.

Differences Among Administrations

When executives' tenure is compared among the various administrations, those appointed by President Roosevelt served longest—in position, in agency, and in government. It would be tempting to assume that Presidents with the longest tenure appointed the executives with the longest tenure, but this does not follow. Truman appointees served for definitely shorter periods than Eisenhower appointees, although Truman was President nearly as long (Table 4.4).

Median tenure of executives appointed by the first three Presidents in this study was about one-quarter to one-third of each Presi-

TABLE 4.4.   *Medians of Position Tenure, Agency Tenure, and Government Tenure, by Administration* [a]

	Tenure Median (Months)		
Administration [b]	Position	Agency	Government
Roosevelt	38	45	52
Truman	22	26	30
Eisenhower	28	32	34
Kennedy [c]	*23*	*28*	*28*

[a] See explanation in Appendix A concerning coverage of tenure tables and computation of tenure and medians.

[b] Tenure figures are not given for the Johnson administration. Such figures would not be significant because only 17 months elapsed between President Johnson's accession and the cut-off date of this study.

[c] Medians in this line were computed only for Kennedy-appointed executives whose tenure ended no later than April 30, 1965 (see Appendix A).

dent's own tenure. By this measure, Eisenhower appointees served longest (Table 4.5).

TABLE 4.5.   *Median Tenure of Federal Political Executives as a Percentage of the Tenure of the Presidents Who Appointed Them*

	President's Tenure (Months)	*Executives' Tenure*		
President [a]		*Position*	*Agency*	*Government*
Roosevelt	145	*26%*	*31%*	*36%*
Truman	93	*24*	*28*	*32*
Eisenhower	96	*29*	*33*	*35*

[a] Similar figures for the Kennedy and Johnson administrations would have little significance, considering the relatively short periods studied and the fact that many appointees were still in office when this study was made.

The general tenure pattern already presented—Roosevelt appointees longest, Eisenhower's next—continues when distributions are examined in Table 4.6. President Roosevelt's appointees had the smallest percentage of short-timers and the largest percentage of longer-service executives. A relatively large proportion of Truman appointees served only two years or less.

TABLE 4.6. *Percentages of Short-Tenure and Long-Tenure Executives, by Administration and Type of Tenure* [a]

Administra-tion	Tenure 2 Years or Less			Tenure Over 3 Years		
	Position	Agency	Govern-ment	Position	Agency	Govern-ment
Roosevelt	33%	30%	23%	52%	57%	64%
Truman	56	47	42	28	34	40
Eisenhower	43	37	34	35	42	46
Kennedy	53	43	43	21	30	31

[a] See explanation in Appendix A concerning coverage of tenure tables and computation of tenure and medians.

Differences Among Agencies

Departments and agencies vary widely in their administrative traditions, their personnel policies, and their relationships with groups in the private economy. These factors cause differences in how long executives stay in their job levels, in their agencies, and in the government. Comparisons of medians among agencies are shown in Chart 4.2 and in Appendix Table F.2.

Commerce Department executives have short tenure (medians are 21 months in the job, 22 in the department, 24 in the government), apparently because of urgent pressures to return to private industry. Tenure at the State Department is also short (23, 26, and 28 months), but here the explanation is more complex. Some executives are short-tenure men from private life. Others are foreign service officers who rotate through executive jobs as well as lower jobs, or through some important jobs (like ambassadorships) not included in the definition of political executive positions. The emergency agencies naturally had low-tenure executives: 17 months in the position, 18 in the agency.

Long-tenure departments include Interior, Post Office, Agriculture, and Treasury—in part reflecting stable patterns of coexistence with their constituencies. Justice tenures are also high, as a result of some long-service attorneys general and assistant attorneys gen-

CHART 4.2. *Median Position Tenure, by Agency*

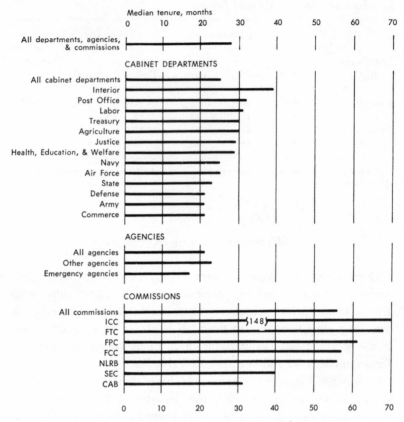

eral. The following table, extracted from Appendix Table F.2, gives the figures.

TENURE MEDIAN (MONTHS)

DEPARTMENT	POSITION	AGENCY	GOVERNMENT
Interior	39	41	41
Post Office	32	35	36
Agriculture	30	34	36
Treasury	30	32	37
Justice	29	37	37

The commissions also had high-tenure figures, which will be analyzed further below.

There were definite differences among the departments in executive mobility (Appendix Table F.2). In each of the military departments executives' tenure in that department and in the government were high, relative to tenure in the position level; thus the Army, Navy, and Air Force executives were more likely to move to other jobs and to other departments, especially to other parts of the Department of Defense. At Treasury, Justice, and Agriculture, executives stayed with the department significantly longer than they stayed in a position level. These relationships among the three types of tenure for the various departments and types of agencies are shown in Chart 4.3. (More refined comparisons of median periods of position tenure, broken down by both agency and position level, may be found in Appendix Table F.3.)

Some of the same general patterns of short-tenure and long-tenure departments show up when distributions rather than medians are examined. Appendix Table F.4 shows that the military departments, Defense, Commerce, and State tend to have more executives with short position tenure and fewer with long tenure. The Departments of Agriculture, Interior, Post Office, and Labor are at the opposite ends of the lists. The "other agencies" are not shown individually in the table because the numbers of persons were so small, but a few specifics should be mentioned: most Veterans Administrators and deputies served over 3 years in their positions. Men in the Bureau of the Budget and the Agency for International Development (including its predecessors) are concentrated in the 1-to-3 year group. Short service, 2 years and less, is characteristic of the executives in the Housing and Home Finance Agency. Those in the General Services Administration and the United States Information Agency had a mixture of long and short position tenure.

When similar comparisons of agency tenure and government tenure are made, the patterns of ranking do not change very much (Appendix Tables F.4, F.5, and F.6). Defense and Commerce head the short-tenure departments, and Interior, Justice, and Post Office have the largest proportions of long-service executives. The Department of the Navy is a notable exception; it has a high proportion of executives with short position tenure, but also a high proportion of executives with long agency tenure and government tenure. Thus Navy executives are likely to change jobs, but tend to stay

CHART 4.3. *Medians of Position Tenure, Agency Tenure, and Government Tenure, by Agency*

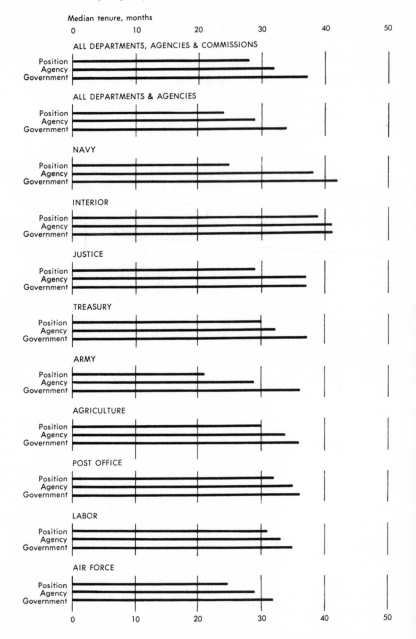

CHART 4.3. *Medians of Position Tenure, Agency Tenure, and Government Tenure, by Agency* (Continued)

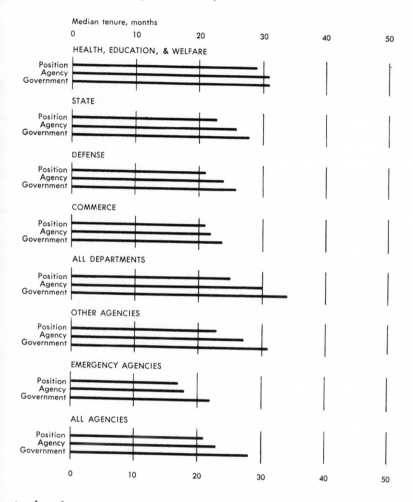

in that department, and in the government, to a greater extent than other executives.

One aspect of tenure in the Department of Defense deserves particular comment. Even though the three military departments and the remainder of the Defense Department were treated as four agencies in this study because of their size and their independent personnel systems, they obviously have a common mission and many occasions for coordination. Some movement of executive personnel naturally has taken place, particularly from the military departments to Defense. Secretaries of Defense James Forrestal and Thomas Gates had served as Under Secretary and Secretary of the Navy; Secretaries Louis Johnson and Robert Lovett had once been assistant secretaries of War. A number of assistant and deputy secretaries of Defense had been in comparable jobs in Army, Navy, or Air Force. Less typical were the cases of Donald Quarles, who went from Defense to Air Force and back to Defense, and of Charles Thomas, who was successively Under Secretary of the Navy, Assistant Secretary of Defense, and Secretary of the Navy.

There were fifteen political executives in the defense departments with multiple appointments and completed government tenure. Their tenure in these departments ranged from 30 to 103 months, with a median of 57—almost 5 years. Their months of service in the defense departments other than in the department where they were first appointed ranged from 9 to 66, with a median of 20 months. Other executives with such multiple appointments and long periods of tenure (for example, Harold Brown, Cyrus Vance) were still serving as this book went to press. Thus such executives contributed more experienced service to the defense activities of the government than is readily apparent from review of the data on position and agency tenure.

Appointments and Tenure of Commissioners

It is worth repeating that regulatory commissions differ from other agencies in two ways important to this study: (1) appointments are for a fixed, statutory term of years; (2) the commissions are bipartisan either by law, or, in the case of the National Labor Relations Board, by usage.

The commissioners, as already noted, served in their jobs much longer than did the other political executives: a median of 56 months, compared with 25 (Chart 4.2).[12] This median of between 4 and 5

---

[12] Neither agency tenure nor government tenure will be discussed in this section. Except in the case of the Federal Trade Commission, so few commis-

years of service is actually less than one full term on any of the commissions (the terms range from 5 to 7 years). Table 4.7 shows that the median tenure of Civil Aeronautics Board members was less than half of one term, while that of Interstate Commerce commissioners approached two full terms. Only in the ICC and the Federal Power Commission did medians exceed a full term.

TABLE 4.7. *Commissioners' Median Position Tenure and Statutory Terms, by Commission*

Commission	Date of Creation	Statutory Term (Months)	Median Position Tenure (Months)	*Tenure as Percentage of Term*
All seven	—	—	56	—
Civil Aeronautics Board	1938	72	31	*43%*
Federal Communications Commission	1934	84	57	*68*
Federal Power Commission	1930	60	61	*102*
Federal Trade Commission	1915	84	68	*81*
Interstate Commerce Commission	1887	84	148	*176*
National Labor Relations Board	1935	60	56	*93*
Securities and Exchange Commission	1934	60	40	*67*

A few commissioners (3 percent) served for only half a year or less. Nearly eight times as many (23 percent) served for 8 years or more. Analysis of their tenure shows the greatest concentrations in this over-8-year category; next were 2–3 years (17 percent) and 4–5 (13 percent). Brief periods of tenure (2 years and under) were most prevalent in the Civil Aeronautics Board (34 percent), the Federal Trade Commission (25 percent), and the Securities and Exchange Commission (20 percent). Long periods of service (over 5 years) were found most often in the Interstate Commerce Com-

---

sioners served in other agencies than their own commissions that government tenure differs from position tenure by only negligible amounts. Median position tenure for FTC members was 68 months; their median government tenure was 79 months. Agency tenure is the same as position tenure in all commissions except the Federal Communications Commission, where it differs very little (see Table 4.1, note b).

mission (56 percent), the Federal Trade Commission (33 percent) (which showed an uneven tenure distribution), the Federal Power Commission (30 percent), and the Federal Communications Commission (17 percent).

The marked differences among the seven commissions merit individual case analysis by other researchers. The variations result from a mixture of administrative traditions, relationships with the regulated industries, political pressures, attitudes of the Presidents, and motivations and performance of the commissioners themselves. It is significant that median tenure is longest in the three oldest commissions: ICC, FTC, and FPC.

The age of the commissions may also account in part for the increase in commissioners' tenure from the period covered by Herring's study (Table 4.8). This trend to longer tenure for commis-

TABLE 4.8. *Commissioners' Median Position Tenure, Herring Study and Present Study, by Commission*

Commission	Herring Study (1887-1935) [a]		Present Study (1933-1965)	
	Number of Persons	Median Tenure (Months)	Number of Persons	Median Tenure (Months)
Interstate Commerce Commission	32	82	23	148
Federal Trade Commission	20	38	21	68
Federal Radio (Communications) Commission	12	25 [b]	29	57
Federal Power Commission	3	24 [b]	20	61

[a] E. Pendleton Herring, *Federal Commissioners* (Harvard University Press, 1936), pp. 129-32.
[b] Figures of limited significance because of newness of commission at the time of Herring's study.

sioners contrasts with the opposite trend reported earlier in this chapter (Table 4.3) for under secretaries and assistant secretaries.

The tenure pattern already discussed for all political executives holds true for commissioners too: Roosevelt appointees longest (median 61 months), Eisenhower next (56), then Truman (49) and Kennedy (29). (No Johnson appointees had completed position tenure.) The median tenure for four administrations was 56 months.

When the distribution of months of service is examined in detail, the most striking figure is that 37 percent of the Roosevelt appointees served over 8 years.

Number of Appointments

The tenure of commissioners may also be viewed in another way —how many appointments did they receive? Three commissioners out of every five (59 percent) had no reappointments, and hence served only a partial term or at most one full term (Appendix Table F.7). Doubtless some of the factors that influence reappointments are the same as those affecting length of service. Nevertheless, the commissions with the lowest percentages of reappointments are not necessarily those whose members have the lowest median tenure. Commissioners were most likely to be reappointed to the Interstate Commerce Commission and the Securities and Exchange Commission. Both agencies have maintained generally stable relationships, based on mutual approval, with the regulated industries. Their regulatory policies, moreover, have not developed along partisan lines. Both factors tend to favor commissioners' reappointments. Yet the ICC is a long-tenure commission and SEC short-tenure—facts that suggest the need for further research. One can speculate that outside job opportunities were more frequent and tempting for SEC members.

Reappointments were lowest in the Federal Trade Commission and the National Labor Relations Board. In contrast with ICC and SEC, these two agencies have less stable relationships with less structured industrial complexes. The policies of both FTC and NLRB, furthermore, have been more influenced by partisan Republican or Democratic considerations. It is understandable that these factors reduce the likelihood that members will be reappointed. Reappointments were also low in the Civil Aeronautics Board and the Federal Communications Commission, suggesting dynamic relationships with their clienteles and with interested politicians.

Commissioners are more often reappointed by Presidents of the same political party than of the opposite party (Appendix Table F.7). Of the commissioners covered by this study, 59 percent received no reappointments, 38 percent were reappointed by a President of the same party, and 6 percent by a President of the opposite party. When a new party takes over the presidency, the majority membership of the commissions soon shifts to that party, and this change reduces reappointments of commissioners from the opposite party. The Interstate Commerce Commission ranks highest both in total reappointments and in reappointments made by Presidents of opposite parties—thus reinforcing the pattern of stability in that body. The Federal Trade Commission is lowest in both respects.

A detailed presentation of partial-term appointments and full-term appointments and reappointments appears in Appendix Table F.8. When this information is compared with Herring's data for the two oldest commissions, it is clear that there has been a trend to an increased number of reappointments for commissioners (Appendix Table F.9). This is to be expected, for Table 4.8 has already shown a trend to longer tenure.

Departure from Office

Over half of the commissioners (51 percent) ended their government service through resignation before the end of their terms. They resigned for a wide variety of avowed and actual reasons, but it was not possible in this study to separate the former from the latter. An additional 38 percent were not reappointed at the end of their terms, sometimes for reasons of the President, sometimes for reasons of their own. Nine percent died in office, and 2 percent left upon reaching compulsory retirement age (70).

There were large differences among the commissions, attributable to complex combinations of factors: the nature of the regulatory program, its political sensitivity, nongovernment job opportunities, personal relationships with the President, and many others. Only 24 percent of the Federal Power Commissioners resigned, as compared with 80 percent at the Securities and Exchange Commission. Non-reappointment was the way out for 65 percent of the members of the National Labor Relations Board, but for only 30 percent of the Interstate Commerce commissioners. At both ICC and FPC death removed one commissioner out of five, but no members of the NLRB or the Civil Aeronautics Board died during the period under study. (See Appendix Table F.10 for further details.)

5

Later Careers

WHERE DID THEY GO, both vocationally and geographically? Study of the subsequent activities of 984 of the 1,041 political executives showed that:

55 percent were in private business or professional pursuits;

18 percent were in federal service in some other capacity, in one of the three branches;

12 percent had retired or died;

13 percent were still in office, as of April 30, 1965; and

2 percent were otherwise engaged.[1]

Of those who returned to private life the two most numerous categories were the 21 percent who went back to the same organizations where they had worked before becoming federal political executives, and the 15 percent who went back to their previous professions but who joined or formed new organizations.

More detailed scrutiny of the figures (Table 5.1) shows that the cabinet officers, military secretaries, under secretaries, and general counsel were those who were more likely to go back to their old employers. Men completing service as general counsel and commissioners were those most likely to go into new organizations in their old professions. In many cases this meant moving to a different law firm. Assistant secretaries and deputy administrators remained in

---

[1] See Appendix A for a detailed explanation of tabulations of subsequent careers. Subsequent careers for 57 (5 percent) of the total population could not be determined.

TABLE 5.1. *Subsequent Careers, by Position Level* [a]

Occupation [b]	All Levels	Cabinet Secretary	Military Secretary	Under Secretary	Assistant Secretary	General Counsel	Administrator	Deputy Administrator	Commissioner
Still in office at indicated level	13%	10%	5%	6%	10%	11%	5%	5%	19%
Federal service (other)	18	18	23	20	28	24	21	31	11
Retired or died	12	19	5	6	6	6	11	10	21
Returned to same organization	21	30	36	33	19	27	21	15	12
Returned to business related to federal executive work	3	1	9	4	3	0	3	2	2
Returned to business unrelated to federal executive work	5	5	5	9	6	3	8	7	2
New in business related to federal executive work	3	—	—	1	2	3	7	1	4
New in business unrelated to federal executive work	2	2	—	3	2	—	3	3	3
Same profession, new organization	15	8	14	10	14	20	14	8	20
New profession	3	1	—	1	3	1	4	6	2
Other private	3	4	—	3	3	4	3	5	2
Total private business and professions	55	51	64	64	52	58	63	47	47
Other	2	1	5	3	2	1	1	5	1
Number of persons [c]	984	83	22	144	459	79	76	96	204

[a] Percentages may not add to 100 because of rounding.   [b] See Appendix A for a detailed explanation of tabulations of subsequent careers.

[c] Numbers of persons in individual position levels do not add to the total for all position levels, because a person is counted once in each position level in which he served, but only once in the total for all position levels.

74

federal service in larger proportions, presumably because of advancement to higher executive positions.

Since the Truman and Eisenhower administrations were followed by a party turnover, fewer of their executives had a future in federal service, and more turned to private pursuits—64 and 63 percent, respectively (Appendix Table G.1). The Roosevelt administration showed the largest percentage of executives who remained in federal service (34 percent). The Eisenhower administration had the largest percentage (28) of officials (mainly businessmen) who went back to their old organizations. The Roosevelt and Truman executives were those who had the strongest tendency to join new organizations in their professions. Figures for the Kennedy and Johnson administrations will not bear close analysis because of the large percentage of executives still serving.

The patterns of federal political executives' later careers also differ by department and agency (Appendix Table G.2). A large number (43 percent) of State Department officials stayed in federal service, as ambassadors or in other foreign service capacities. The Department of Justice was likewise high in the federal service category, many of its executives having moved to other political posts or judgeships. The independent agencies, both emergency and other, and the Department of Agriculture followed State and Justice in having a large group of alumni in federal service. At the bottom of the list in this respect were Navy, Defense, the Federal Power Commission, and the Federal Communications Commission.

The departments whose executives showed the strongest tendency to go back to their original employers were Defense, Air Force, Army, Treasury, Commerce, and Health, Education, and Welfare. The first five primarily represent returns to commercial pursuits, the last one to academic fields. Commission members were less likely to go back to previous employers and, as noted above, more inclined to start with different organizations after their government service. However, only 6 percent of the commissioners went into businesses related to their federal service. Finally, retirement and death accounted for the largest percentages of executives in the commissions —except for the shorter tenure ones, the Civil Aeronautics Board and the Securities and Exchange Commission.

The subsequent career patterns of the executives who had worked for large defense contractors[2] did not differ much from those of the total group: 34 percent went back to their old employers; 34 percent moved to other careers in private industry; 14 percent were still in office; 7 percent retired or died; and 10 percent were miscellaneous or not determined.

Location of Later Careers

The final analysis in this study was an effort to see whether executives changed their geographic locations after their periods of federal service. The results are not particularly conclusive.

Large numbers of these officials, as pointed out in Chapter 2, had their principal prior occupations in Washington (28 percent) and New York City (14 percent). Similar percentages prevail for location of subsequent careers: 30 percent in Washington and 17 percent in New York.[3] About a quarter of the executives went back to the states they worked before they became federal political executives, and a few less (17 percent) located their new careers elsewhere.[4]

Table 5.2 shows the locations of these later careers, broken down by agencies. The stay-in-Washington contingent was led by executives of the Justice Department, the emergency agencies, and the Federal Trade Commission. The parade to New York was headed by men from the Air Force, the Securities and Exchange Commission, and, to a lesser degree, the Army and Treasury. The high percentage of "elsewhere's" from the State Department results from further overseas assignments for noncareer diplomats. The highest percentage of executives going back to the state where they had worked before was from the Interior Department. Other large groups of "returnees" were from Defense, Navy, Commerce, and the Civil Aeronautics Board.

---

[2] See above, Chap. 3, p. 38.

[3] See Appendix A for a detailed explanation of tabulations of subsequent careers.

[4] These percentages do not include those who returned to occupations or began new careers located in Washington and New York City.

Agency	Washington D.C. 30%	New York City 17%	Same State as Principal Prior Occupation [b] 23%	Elsewhere 17%	Retired or Died 13%	Number of Persons [c] 866
All departments, agencies, and commissions	*30*	*17*	*23*	*17*	*13*	*866*
State	22	16	9	44	9	116
Treasury	33	24	22	12	8	49
Defense	32	18	38	4	9	56
Army	25	27	30	7	11	44
Navy	26	14	34	6	20	35
Air Force	17	41	21	14	7	29
Justice	55	16	25	3	—	87
Post Office	39	11	23	11	16	44
Interior	37	3	40	6	14	35
Agriculture	40	3	23	26	9	35
Commerce	25	17	34	17	7	59
Labor	33	14	22	19	11	36
Health, Education, and Welfare	20	20	28	24	8	25
All departments	*30*	*17*	*25*	*18*	*10*	*607*
Emergency agencies	47	17	20	13	3	60
Other agencies	34	13	16	23	15	88
All agencies	*38*	*14*	*18*	*19*	*10*	*145*
All departments and agencies	*31*	*17*	*24*	*18*	*10*	*721*
Civil Aeronautics Board	36	14	32	14	5	22
Federal Communications Commission	38	8	12	8	35	26
Federal Power Commission	19	10	24	10	38	21
Federal Trade Commission	55	5	10	—	30	20
Interstate Commerce Commission	26	9	13	—	52	23
National Labor Relations Board	40	5	15	20	20	20
Securities and Exchange Commission	26	40	17	9	9	35
All commissions	*33*	*15*	*17*	*9*	*26*	*163*

[a] Categories are mutually exclusive. See Appendix A for a detailed explanation of tabulation of subsequent careers.   [b] Excluding Washington and New York.   [c] Numbers of persons in individual agency groupings (such as State, Emergency agencies) do not add to the subtotals (All departments, All commissions) or the total persons, because a person is counted once in each agency grouping in which he served, but only once in a subtotal or total grouping.

6

General Findings, Interpretations, and Leads

"IS THAT GOOD OR BAD?" is a question that can be asked about almost every statistic in the preceding five chapters, and the answer will depend on the values of the reader. The data in this book may give reassurance to patriots, corroboration to sociologists, workload to graduate students, and pause to politicians.

These 1000-plus executives, given 1500-plus appointments over 32 years to some 180 top positions, are a well-qualified group. Considering how different the jobs are, it is astonishing how much alike the men are.[1] But this is not so astonishing when the major requirements of the jobs are considered—incisiveness, ability to negotiate, public presence, ability to analyze and synthesize, and all the rest. They have had to meet problems that were shifting and growing in this period that covered a major depression, several recessions, World War II and the postwar adjustments, the Korean conflict, and the cold war. Such problems sometimes made it necessary to recruit executives with specialized qualifications, and sometimes put new and unusual burdens on the executives already on the job.

How Representative? And of Whom?

Various groups in the population are overrepresented—naturally. Federal political executives tend to be "city boys," Easterners, Protestants, well-educated, and middle-aged. Such executives have fitted

---

[1] Not to mention the twelve ladies.

this pattern for years. Trends are visible in the present study, but not very strong trends. The educational level has risen a little, as it has for other leaders. The proportion of Catholics has increased. The commissioners are a little younger when appointed and the other executives a little older.

There were some differences among administrations, as earlier chapters have brought out, particularly between the Eisenhower and Democratic administrations. The Eisenhower executives were more likely to come from the central states, small towns, and big cities (other than New York and Washington); to have attended well-known prep schools; to be Protestants; and to be older at time of appointment.

Occupationally, these executives come mostly from government service, law, and business—not only that, but from big government, big law, big business. Educators are also present, but scientists and engineers are relatively rare. Again, there were differences by presidency, with Truman appointing more career public servants and Eisenhower more businessmen.

Federal political executives are not representative of the general population, or even of the educated, financially stable population. They are representative of persons who have an affinity for public service and demonstrated ability to run large enterprises or to give specialized aid to those who run them. The recruitment and selection process helps assure this.[2] Candidates for executive posts are selected primarily for their capacities for the job to be filled, their attitudes toward the President's programs, and their ability to work with others. Recruiting and screening activities filter through tangled networks of personal, political, and professional acquaintanceships. Thus similarities in background must be expected.

These patterns can, if one wishes, be merged into a picture of a dominant, self-seeking "political directorate." Such a picture can be obliterated with barbed, well-documented whimsy or with reassur-

[2] See Dean E. Mann with Jameson W. Doig, *The Assistant Secretaries: Problems and Processes of Appointment* (Brookings Institution, 1965), esp. pp. 64–86.

ance that the need for "The Establishment" has passed.[3] Perhaps more persuasively, the nonestablishment citizen can take comfort in the factors that restrain political executives from behaving like trade associations or ward committees. For one thing, there are diversity and disagreement within their unity. For another, they are daily observed, even assailed, by the news media, Congress, and lobbies. Conspiracy is difficult under these conditions.

These executives were hired to run the government, and the recruitment process, generally speaking, has been an effort to get the best people for that purpose, even if their unrepresentativeness of the general population may result in occasional strains. Yet the executives *are* representative of persons with legal, managerial, and analytical skills in American society. A case can be made that the leaders of the bureaucracies are more representative, more responsive to public concerns, than are members of Congress—more likely to be concerned with the breadth and complexity of public policy issues and less inclined to support parochial pressures of narrow interest groups.[4]

How Prepared?

Federal service was an old story to a very large majority of the federal political executives, according to the statistical evidence in Chapter 3. Sixty-three percent of the appointees had had federal administrative service—a median of five years—at time of first appointment. Thirty-eight percent had backgrounds in other levels of government. These high proportions could be both good and bad: good, because of the executives' experience, contacts, and motivation; bad, because they may tend to accept governmental usages that newcomers might challenge. However interpreted, the figures suggest that previous literature has overemphasized the "amateur

[3] C. Wright Mills, *The Power Elite* (Oxford University Press, 1956), pp. 225–41; Richard H. Rovere, *The American Establishment* . . . (Harcourt, Brace & World, 1962), pp. 3–21; Joseph Kraft, "The End of the Establishment," *Washington Post*, March 2, 1966.

[4] See Norton E. Long, "Bureaucracy and Constitutionalism," *The Polity*, edited by Charles Press (Rand McNally, 1962), pp. 64–76.

standing" of federal political executives, that is, their lack of knowledge of the political and administrative setting in which they are to work.[5]

On the whole, the natural hypothesis that previous government service would be good preparation for political executive positions was supported by the evaluations in the companion volume to this study:

> Except for those in elective politics, government officials as a group were considered to be better executives than men who came exclusively from the private sector. . . . [M]en from private occupations who had also had a considerable background in government work were rated higher than those with no public service experience at all.

The evaluations also show that executives with less than two years of government administrative service "did not measure up to their colleagues with longer terms in government.[6]

This preparation through other public service also had immediacy, for 69 percent of the appointees to federal political executive jobs were in other government positions just before their appointments.

It is fair to infer that many of the practicing lawyers and businessmen who became political executives were partly prepared for their work both by the scope of their private responsibilities and by contacts with the federal government. The only evidence in this study on the latter point, however, is that some 12 percent of the executives in defense-related agencies had worked for defense contractors. There are obviously dangers in using this source of recruitment that may outweigh the advantages—actual or potential conflict of interest, disputes with competing industries, loss of public confidence. These equities must be evaluated by the President and the department head in the light of all the program factors involved. A similar problem is raised (with equally mixed answers) by the appointment of commissioners who have worked in the industry or function regulated by the commission.

⁵ There is some emphasis of this point in Commission on Organization of the Executive Branch of the Government, *Personnel and Civil Service* (1955), and *Task Force Report on Personnel and Civil Service* (1955); and in Marver H. Bernstein, *The Job of the Federal Executive* (Brookings Institution, 1958).

⁶ Mann, *The Assistant Secretaries*, pp. 247, 248.

More broadly, any clientele group provides a logical source of interested, proven executives whose value to the government may be impaired by implied or real conflicts between public and private policy.

How Long Retained?

It is good that federal political executives are as well prepared as they are because they do not stay in their jobs very long. The median job tenure of two to three years for executives (other than commissioners) gives a man little enough time between the end of his orientation—if it ever ends—and the start of his next job.[7] The situation is somewhat improved by the fact that many go on to other executive positions—recall that their median government tenure is nearly three years. This is still a short time, considering the difficulty and responsibility of the work.

Little can be done about some of the factors causing short tenure: crushing workload, administrative frustrations, difficulties with the news media or the legislative branch, family problems. Progress has been made on one item—executive pay levels—although true comparability with high salaries in the private sector is never likely to be achieved. Executives could be given more feeling of progress and accomplishment, particularly through better orientation and supervision.[8]

Still more difficult is the factor of interrupted careers elsewhere. Business executives who stay in government more than two or three years fear loss of fringe benefits and of their places in the pecking order. Lawyers fear loss of clients. These executives know very well that any personnel structure abhors a vacuum. The longer they stay in Washington, the harder it may be for them to gain a position as good as one they would have attained if they had stayed at home. This disadvantage is reduced by the advantages of prestige,

[7] Though the statistics in Chap. 4 refute the statement of one observer close enough to know better that "assistant secretaries come to Washington for one social season."

[8] See discussion of reasons for executives' leaving in Mann, *The Assistant Secretaries*, pp. 204–27, esp. pp. 211–17.

contacts, and knowledge they have gained as federal political executives. The President and the department heads (mostly long-tenure men themselves) could try to influence other executives to see a longer-run future for themselves in federal posts. White House executive recruiters could also try to persuade corporation presidents and heads of law firms to let their men stay in Washington for longer periods without prejudice to their careers. This might reduce the percentage (now 55) of those who move to private employment and increase the percentage (31) of those who stay in federal service.

Even with maximum efforts to increase the executive tenure figures, there is little danger that these officials will go stale on the job. The incentives for them to return to, or begin, private careers are so powerful that there will inevitably be plenty of room for fresh talent.

How Widely Used?

Most of the executives (91 percent) were one-agency men, and a large majority (63 percent) were one-appointment men. Chapter 4 noted a tendency to promote assistant secretaries and others to other federal political executive jobs.[9] These officials would probably be more valuable to the government if they served in more than one job and in more than one agency—just as in the case of higher civil servants.[10]

The trouble is that the typical political executive doesn't stay around long enough to do justice to even one job. It seems more important at present to lengthen tenure than to increase intragovernment mobility—but there should be strong long-run efforts to do both.

[9] Note also that 37 percent of the under secretaries and assistant secretaries studied in the companion volume moved to other federal posts; *ibid.*, p. 298.
[10] "Every job in a different organization gives the employee a new body of knowledge, affects his skills, and adds a new perspective. All these qualifications he takes with him to future jobs, which are benefited by the understanding he has gained. Increased mobility is basic to the development of the truly superior executive or professional in federal service." David T. Stanley, *The Higher Civil Service* (Brookings Institution, 1964), p. 89.

How Little Is Known?

Both the present study and *The Assistant Secretaries* have produced a large volume of statistics and case material from which trends, successes, and problems have been identified. Yet both studies, true to the breeder-reactor nature of social science research, show gaps in knowledge and needs for further investigation.

Some of the related studies suggested by the work done so far are these:

Further research on the performance of federal political executives, including some evaluations from outside the executive branch. Comparative evaluations of performance of the more mobile and less mobile executives would be desirable.

Attitudinal studies on representativeness to determine the strength of their loyalties to their home regions, their commercial employers, their race, their religions.

Studies tracing the career progress of individual executives who have moved between the public and private sectors to determine how government experience has aided private career development, and vice versa.

Detailed analysis of potential conflict-of-interest strains in cases of executives selected from defense contractors, regulated industries, and other clientele groups.

Individual depth studies of reasons for longer political executive tenure among the various departments and agencies.

Most readers probably have lengthened this list before they came to it. In the complex milieu of federal political executives the varied vectors of power, loyalty, ambition, conscience, and sheer chance will always assure that the unanswerable questions outnumber the answerable. Yet what is known gives grounds for much satisfaction, despite the uncertainties, the problems, and even the failures. Federal political executives have brought impressive talents to public service, and as always they will be needed more than they are appreciated.

APPENDIXES

APPENDIX A

Methodology

Agency and Position Coverage

Three groups of federal political executives are included in this study. Almost all are filled by presidential appointment with the advice and consent of the Senate.

DEPARTMENTS. The first group includes positions at the assistant secretary level and above in the ten cabinet departments[1] and the three military departments, excluding positions with the title "Special Assistant" and those reserved for career employees by statute.

The War and Navy Departments were cabinet departments until they became military departments within the National Military Establishment—later the Department of Defense—in accordance with the National Security Act of 1947. The Department of the Air Force was established as a military department at that time, taking over the functions of the Army Air Forces of the old War Department. Army, Navy, and Air Force are discussed and tabulated as military departments throughout this book. (In data tabulated by agency, the War Department is treated as predecessor of the Department of the Army). The Department of Defense exclusive of the military departments is treated as a cabinet department.

Data concerning the Department of Health, Education, and Welfare, established as a cabinet department in 1953, include its predecessor, the Federal Security Agency, established in 1939.

---

[1] The Department of Housing and Urban Development was created after the research for this study was completed. Its predecessor, the Housing and Home Finance Agency, is included as one of the noncabinet agencies. The Department of Transportation was established while this book was in press.

The several position levels within this group are:

Secretary (or Attorney General or Postmaster General);

Under Secretary (or Deputy Secretary, Deputy Attorney General, Deputy Postmaster General, and Under Secretaries with specific functional titles such as Under Secretary for Transportation);

Assistant Secretary (or Assistant Attorney General, Assistant Postmaster General, Solicitor General, Assistant Solicitor General, Counselor [of the Department of State], The Assistant to the Attorney General[2], Director and Deputy Director of Defense Research and Engineering, Deputy Under Secretary, and Assistant Secretaries and Deputy Under Secretaries with specific functional titles, such as Assistant Secretary for Legislation);

General Counsel (or such equivalent titles as Solicitor, Legal Adviser, or Department Counselor [of the Department of the Army]).

AGENCIES. The second group includes the top two positions in selected noncabinet agencies. Agencies were selected on the basis of the following criteria:

1. They resemble the major departments in their public visibility, their major responsibilities in carrying out important governmental programs, and in their relationships with important groups in the society.

2. They have a single executive and a continuing deputy.

3. They have enough continuity over time, including predecessor agencies, to provide a reasonably adequate number of executives for analysis.

These agencies (and their predecessors) include:[3]

Agency for International Development and its predecessors: International Cooperation Administration (1955–1961); Foreign Operations Administration (1953–1955); Technical Cooperation Administration (1953); Mutual Security Agency (1951–1953); Economic Cooperation Administration (1948–1951); Foreign Economic Administration (1943–1945);

---

[2] A position in existence from 1933 to 1951 with functions equivalent to an assistant secretary of a cabinet department. Normally "Assistant to . . ." positions are excluded.

[3] For statistical analysis several agencies have been grouped together in tabulations by agency. See p. 93 of this appendix for details.

Housing and Home Finance Agency and its predecessor, National Housing Agency (1942–1947);

United States Information Agency and its predecessor, Office of War Information (1942–1945);

The following depression agencies: Federal Emergency Administration of Public Works (1933–1943); Federal Emergency Relief Administration (1933–1938); National Recovery Administration (1933–1935); Works Progress Administration (1935–1939);

The following war and war planning agencies: Office of Emergency Planning; Office of Civil and Defense Mobilization (1958–1961); Office of Defense Mobilization (1950–1958); Federal Civil Defense Administration (1950–1958); Defense Production Administration (1951–1953); Office of War Mobilization and Reconversion (1944–1946); Office of War Mobilization (1943–1944); War Production Board (1942–1945); Economic Stabilization Agency (1950–1953); Office of Price Administration (1941–1946);

Bureau of the Budget;

General Services Administration;

Veterans Administration;

Federal Loan Agency (1939–1942);

Federal Works Agency (1939–1949).

COMMISSIONS. The third group includes commissioners of seven independent regulatory agencies:

Civil Aeronautics Board;

Federal Communications Commission;

Federal Power Commission;

Federal Trade Commission;

Interstate Commerce Commission;

National Labor Relations Board;

Securities and Exchange Commission.

The present study excludes:

The Federal Maritime Board, which has been part of the Department of Commerce since 1950, but from 1936 until 1950 was the United States Maritime Commission, an independent agency;

The Board of Governors of the Federal Reserve System, which is financed by member banks, not out of appropriations, and whose policy functions are unique;[4]

[4] See Marver H. Bernstein, *Regulating Business by Independent Commission* (Princeton University Press, 1955), p. 8 n.

The United States Tariff Commission, whose functions are investigatory rather than regulatory;

The Federal Radio Commission, a predecessor of the Federal Communications Commission (1927–1934).[5]

Data for members of the seven commissions included in the present study who served during the period 1935–1960 were collected and arranged in preliminary form by Dean Marver H. Bernstein of the Woodrow Wilson School of Public and International Affairs, Princeton University. The project staff expanded this number to include all appointments to these commissions by President Franklin Roosevelt, and appointments by Presidents Kennedy and Johnson through April 30, 1965.

Administration Coverage

The study includes all persons appointed or reappointed to the above positions by Presidents Roosevelt, Truman, Eisenhower, Kennedy, and Johnson between March 4, 1933, and April 30, 1965. A person was considered to have been reappointed to a department or agency position if he remained in office more than six months after the new President took office, except for commissioner reappointments which are formal actions requiring Senate approval. Recess appointments withdrawn by an outgoing President are not included.

Data Collection

Master lists by agency, position, and administration were prepared for all persons serving in positions covered in this study.

For each person on the master lists, data were collected on:

Year of birth
Type of precollege education
Type of undergraduate education (schools and degrees)
Type of graduate education (schools and degrees)
Level of education
Political affiliation
Religious preference

[5] The last three agencies named were included in E. Pendleton Herring's *Federal Commissioners* (Harvard University Press, 1936).

For each appointment on the master lists (some persons had more than one appointment), the following data were collected:

Title of position
Dates of service in position
Principal occupation before appointment, including:
    Location (state and size of city) of principal occupation before appointment
    Size and type of organization (if employed in business or universities)
    Classification of industry in which employed
Secondary occupation before appointment
Position immediately before appointment
Prior federal public service (type and length of service)
Other prior public service (type and length of service)
Occupation after appointment
Location (state) of occupation after appointment
Any federal service at the federal political executive level after this appointment (length of service)

Biographical information for these persons was obtained primarily from standard sources, such as *Who's Who in America, Who's Who in World Jewry,* and *Current Biography,* from biographical releases from the individual departments and agencies, and from other federal records. It was possible to assemble basic biographical data for all but nine of the executives. Data were essentially complete for about 95 percent of the persons studied.

Coding

Detailed coding instructions were prepared for categorizing the data. The following are additional sources which were used in placing data in proper coding categories.

For the size of cities:
    Bureau of the Census publications and the *World Almanac*
For types of secondary schools:
    Directory of Secondary Day Schools, 1951–52
    Catholic Secondary Schools in USA
For industrial and business classifications:
    Fortune Directory of the 500 Largest U. S. Industrial Corporations

Polk's Bank Directory

Standard Industrial Classification Manual published by the Bureau of the Budget

Lists of the largest defense contractors supplied by the Department of Defense

List of the largest investment firms supplied by the Investment Bankers Association of America

One coding form (combining personal data and relevant appointment data) was completed for one person's continuous service in each federal political executive position.

Tabulation

Information from the coding forms was placed on punch cards and tabulated by National Analysts, Inc., from tabulation specifications designed by the authors.

CODING EXECUTIVES IN SUBPOPULATIONS. The reader has observed the variety of N's (numbers or subpopulations) used in tabulations in this book. The need for this complexity grew out of the fact that over 200 persons in the population studied served in more than one appointment, position, agency, or administration. In tabulating various characteristics, it was necessary to count each person once, and no person more than once, in the appropriate category.

Example:

Assume that the percentages of persons who have bachelor's degrees are being tabulated for the entire population, and by position, by agency, and by administration. Assume further that John Doe served as Assistant Secretary of State and Assistant Secretary of Commerce under President Truman, as Under Secretary of Labor and Secretary of Labor under President Kennedy, and continued as Secretary of Labor under President Johnson.

In determining the N's which are to be used in computing the percentages of persons with bachelor's degrees, Mr. Doe will be counted as follows:

Only once when the total population of persons with bachelor's degrees is tabulated;

Only once as an assistant secretary, and once each as under secretary and secretary when holders of bachelor's degrees are being tabulated by position level;

Once each in the Departments of State, Commerce, and Labor, when the degree holders are being tabulated by agency;

Once each in the Truman, Kennedy, and Johnson administrations, when the tabulation is by administration.

Obviously the percentages are misleading if Doe is omitted from any of these categories or is counted more than once in any one of them.

Thus such tabulating breaks and N units as the following were determined:

Break: Total persons
Unit: 1 person in this study
Each person in the study is counted only once.

Break: Persons, by agency
Unit: 1 person in 1 agency break
Each person is counted once in each agency break in which he served. (See the note on agency break below.)

Break: Persons, by administration
Unit: 1 person serving in a specific President's administration
Each person is counted once in each President's administration in which he served, either as an appointment or as a reappointment.

Break: Total appointments
Unit: 1 appointment (or 1 reappointment)
Each appointment and each reappointment is counted once.

Break: Appointments, by agency
Unit: 1 appointment or 1 reappointment in 1 agency
Each appointment and each reappointment is counted once in each agency in which it belongs.

(Other breaks and units are defined in the Glossary, Appendix B, and in footnotes to the appropriate tables.)

AGENCY GROUPINGS. In the tabulations by agency, some agency breaks include more than one agency. This was done for two reasons:

1. Such groupings provide a relatively continuous group of people appointed to serve in similar areas of governmental administration, comparable to the grouping of all people appointed to any one department. Thus some agency breaks include a current department and its predecessors.

2. Such groupings provide an N large enough to permit statistical analysis. So many of the "depression" and "war and war planning" agencies, although of major importance in carrying out governmental programs, existed for such a short time that they could not sepa-

rately provide a significant number of persons or appointments. Therefore, these two groups were combined to form the broader category "emergency agencies." The remaining noncabinet and noncommission agencies were also grouped together as "other agencies" for this same reason.

TENURE TABULATIONS—EXECUTIVES IN OFFICE ON APRIL 30, 1965. Tables which concern position tenure only include all instances of federal political executive service in which a person completed his tenure in a position by April 30, 1965, plus a few instances in which such tenure was completed between that date and the time these statistics were tabulated. Tables which compare position tenure with agency tenure and government tenure include tenure data only for persons whose government service as a federal political executive had been completed by April 30, 1965, or by the time these statistics were tabulated. Thus an executive who had gone from one political executive position to another and who was still in a political executive position at the end of this study was included in the first category of tables, but not the second. Because of these differences in coverage, position tenure medians may differ slightly from one category of tables to the other.

There may be slight differences in medians used in these comparative tables, in addition to those explained above, since medians in comparative tables are grouped and those for tables which consider only one type of tenure are ungrouped.

CREDITING OF POLITICAL EXECUTIVE SERVICE IN GOVERNMENT TENURE TABULATIONS. Thirty-four of the executives studied served not only in the departments or agencies listed above but also as full-time members of one or more of nineteen boards or commissions not included in this study. Such service was included in government tenure tabulations because of its similarity in some respects to service in the departments and agencies. Members of these boards and commissions were appointed by the President and confirmed by the Senate and were in policy-making positions. The boards and commissions are: Atomic Energy Commission; Equal Employment Opportunity Commission; Export-Import Bank (Board of Directors); Federal Coal Mine Safety Board of Review; Federal Deposit Insurance Corporation; Federal Home Loan Bank Board; Federal Maritime Commission; Federal Radio Commission; Federal Reserve Board; Foreign Claims Settlement Commission of the United States; Indian

Claims Commission; National Mediation Board; National Wage Stabilization Board; National War Labor Board (public members only); Railroad Retirement Board; Renegotiation Board; United States Civil Service Commission; United States Shipping Board; and United States Tariff Commission.

TENURE TABULATIONS—MULTIPLE APPOINTMENTS. The method of tabulating tenure in cases of multiple appointments should be noted. Tenure in a second (or subsequent) administration, agency, or position level is credited additionally to the administration, agency, or position level in which the executive was earlier appointed.

Examples:

1. Richard Roe serves 24 months as Assistant Secretary of Commerce in the Roosevelt administration and continues for 18 months more in the Truman administration. He has no more political executive service. Under the definition of reappointments, he is considered a Truman appointee after he has served for six months in that administration. His position, agency, and government tenure are all shown as 42 months under Roosevelt and 18 months under Truman.

2. Sidney Smoe serves under Kennedy for 20 months as Assistant Secretary of the Navy, then 7 months as Assistant Secretary of the Treasury. He has no other political executive service. His position and agency tenures are 20 months in Navy and 7 in Treasury; his government tenure, tabulated by agency, is 27 months credited to Navy and 7 to Treasury.

3. Thomas Toe serves 11 months as Assistant Secretary of Defense, 13 as Deputy Secretary of Defense, and 21 as Secretary of Defense. He has no other political executive service. His position tenure is 11 months as assistant secretary, 13 as under secretary, and 21 as cabinet secretary. His agency tenure and government tenure, tabulated by position level, are 45 months credited in the assistant secretary category, 34 months in the under secretary category, and 21 months in the cabinet secretary category.

4. A much more complex illustration—Walter Woe is appointed by President Roosevelt as Assistant Secretary of State for 10 months, then as Assistant Secretary of Agriculture for 6 months, then as Under Secretary of Labor. After he serves 1 month as Under Secretary of Labor, President Truman takes office, and Woe then serves 8 more months in that position. President Truman then appoints him Secretary of State, which position he holds for 14 months. He has no other political executive service. His tenure is tabulated in the following ways:

Position tenure, tabulated by administration
    Roosevelt—10 months assistant secretary (State)
             6 months assistant secretary (Agriculture)
             9 months under secretary   (Labor)
    Truman — 8 months under secretary   (Labor)
             14 months cabinet secretary (State)
Position tenure, tabulated by agency
    State   —10 months assistant secretary
             14 months cabinet secretary
    Agriculture— 6 months assistant secretary
    Labor   — 9 months under secretary
Position tenure, tabulated by position level
    Assistant secretary—10 months (State)
    Assistant secretary— 6 months (Agriculture)
    Under secretary   — 9 months (Labor)
    Cabinet secretary —14 months (State)
Agency tenure, tabulated by administration
    Roosevelt—24 months (State)
             6 months (Agriculture)
             9 months (Labor)
    Truman — 8 months (Labor)
             14 months (State)
Agency tenure, tabulated by agency
    State   —24 months
    Agriculture— 6 months
    Labor   — 9 months
Agency tenure, tabulated by position level
    Assistant secretary—24 months (State)
    Assistant secretary— 6 months (Agriculture)
    Under secretary   — 9 months (Labor)
    Cabinet   secretary —14 months (State)
Government tenure, tabulated by administration
    Roosevelt—39 months
    Truman —22 months
Government tenure, tabulated by agency
    State   —39 months
    Agriculture—29 months
    Labor   —23 months
[Government tenure was not tabulated by position level]

This practice of crediting subsequent tenure to the administration, agency, or position level where earlier appointed as an executive raises the question: How is political executive service before appointment in the category under analysis credited? Answer: Such prior service is counted as part of "prior federal administrative service" (discussed in Chapter 3).

"SUBSEQUENT CAREER" TABULATIONS. In tabulations for all executives in this study, the nature of a person's career after the last appointment covered by the study is tabulated. In the breaks by position level, administration, or agency, the career after the last appointment in that position level, administration, or agency is tabulated.

Example:

Dean Rusk served as an Assistant Secretary of State under Truman from 1949 to 1952, then as President of the Rockefeller Foundation from 1952 to 1961. In 1961 he was appointed by President Kennedy as Secretary of State and was still in office under President Johnson on April 30, 1965. In tabulations by position level, Rusk's Rockefeller Foundation position is counted as his occupation after his assistant secretary position, and he is shown as "still in office" for the cabinet secretary category. In tabulations by administration, the Rockefeller job is tabulated for the Truman administration, and Rusk is shown as "still in office" for the Kennedy and Johnson administrations. In tabulations by agency, he is counted as "still in office" at the Department of State.

Similar rules apply to the tabulation of location of subsequent careers.

APPENDIX B

Glossary

AGENCY—used most often to mean a single government department, commission, or noncabinet agency. However, the term AGENCIES is sometimes used to mean the specific noncabinet agencies covered in this study, as contrasted with military departments, cabinet departments, and regulatory commissions. *See also* AGENCY BREAK and AGENCY TENURE.

AGENCY BREAK—a grouping of appointments or persons, by agency to which appointed. Individual groupings (with examples in parentheses) used in this book are:

1. A single cabinet department (State);
2. A single military department (Air Force);
3. A military department and its predecessor cabinet department (Army and War);
4. A cabinet department and its predecessor agency (Health, Education, and Welfare and the Federal Security Agency);
5. A group of related agencies (all emergency agencies);
6. A group of unrelated agencies (all agencies other than emergency and cabinet predecessor agencies);
7. A single regulatory commission (Federal Communications Commission);
8. An agency and its predecessor agencies (United States Information Agency and Office of War Information);
9. A single agency (General Services Administration).

AGENCY TENURE—includes one person's service at the federal political executive level in one agency and its predecessor.

APPOINTMENT—an appointment by the President or agency head to a

99

specific federal political executive position. The three types of appointment and their respective beginning dates are:

1. A formal action in which a new person is appointed to a position, beginning the day the appointee takes the oath of office and enters the job;
2. A formal action in which the same person is reappointed to the same position, beginning at the start of the term of office to which the person is reappointed (commissioners only);
3. A case in which an appointee of a previous administration is held over six months or more in a succeeding administration beginning when the new President takes office (this category does not apply to commissioners).

The last two types of appointment are also called REAPPOINTMENTS.

CABINET DEPARTMENT—one of the ten cabinet departments as of 1965, plus the War and Navy Departments preceding the National Security Act of 1947. (The Department of Housing and Urban Development was established after April 30, 1965, the cut-off date of this study.)

COMMISSIONER—a person appointed or reappointed between March 1933 and April 1965 as a member of one of the seven commissions included in this study.

COMMISSION-RELATED INDUSTRY—an industry whose primary business is within a function or a segment of the economy regulated by a specific federal regulatory commission.

DEFENSE CONTRACTOR—one of the largest defense contractors in a relevant time period. For the first Truman administration, the 100 largest prime contractors during World War II are used. For the second Truman and both Eisenhower administrations, and the first year of the Kennedy administration, a list prepared by the Department of Defense entitled "One Hundred Companies and Affiliates Listed According to Net Value of Prime Contract Awards," covering the period July 1950 through June 1956, and published April 10, 1957, is used. For the rest of the Kennedy and the Johnson administrations, an "Index of 100 Parent Companies Which with Their Subsidiaries Received the Largest Dollar Values of Military Prime Contract Awards in Fiscal Year 1963," prepared by the Department of Defense, is used.

FEDERAL ADMINISTRATIVE SERVICE—includes time served in (1) political executive positions, (2) full-time administrative positions in the executive, legislative, and judicial branches of the federal government, and (3) professonal military service. It does not include service as a legislator or judge, or nonprofessional military or part-time service.

FEDERAL POLITICAL EXECUTIVE—a person who has served in one of the cabinet department, military department, agency, or commission positions covered in this study.

GOVERNMENT TENURE—includes one person's full-time service in any of the positions covered in this study or, in the case of 34 executives in the study, as a member of one or more of the boards or commissions listed on p. 94. Membership on any of these boards or commissions was considered to be service at the federal political executive level if it met the following criteria:

1. The commission is multi-headed;
2. The commission is the head of a federal agency;
3. Members of the commission are appointed by the President and confirmed by the Senate for a term of a specific number of years, or at the pleasure of the President;
4. Membership on the commission is a full-time job.

Tenure in commissions not meeting these criteria is not included.

MILITARY DEPARTMENT—one of the three departments—Army, Navy, and Air Force—established as part of the National Military Establishment (later the Department of Defense) in accordance with the National Security Act of 1947. Before that Act, War and Navy existed as separate cabinet departments.

POLITICAL PARTY AFFILIATION—specific mention in a standard biographical reference of a person's identification with a national party.

POSITION LEVEL—a grouping of several federal political executive jobs which are at approximately the same rank within the federal government. There are eight position levels in this study: cabinet secretary, military secretary, under secretary, assistant secretary, general counsel, administrator, deputy administrator, and commissioner. (See Appendix A for the specific titles included within these position level breaks.)

POSITION TENURE—includes one person's completed service in a specific federal political executive job (for example, continuous service in one specific assistant secretary position).

PRINCIPAL OCCUPATION—type of primary occupational experience (such as banker, federal administrator) based on the length of service and its proximity to federal political executive service. (Principal occupation is not determined by formal training; many persons with law degrees, for example, had principal occupations other than law.)

REAPPOINTMENT—*See under* APPOINTMENT.

RELIGIOUS PREFERENCE—specific mention in a standard biographical reference of a person's identification with a religious denomination.

SECONDARY OCCUPATION—type of occupational experience, other than that considered to be a person's principal occupation, of sufficient length (a minimum of three years) and importance to be mentioned as additional occupational experience. Usually the time spent is less than that in a principal occupation and occurs earlier, but these are not absolute criteria.

SUBSEQUENT CAREER—a person's principal occupational experience after he serves as a federal political executive. It is obviously impossible to know in many cases in what field an executive will remain when he has recently left federal political executive service. The results of this study are based on the considered judgment of the authors, but not on any mathematical formula which requires that an individual serve in a position a given number of years to make it a career. In some cases, particularly for Kennedy and Johnson appointees, a person's subsequent career is only a position which he may leave at any time.

TOTAL ADMINISTRATIVE SERVICE—includes FEDERAL ADMINISTRATIVE SERVICE (*see* definition above) and service in administrative positions at the state and local levels; it does not include international service.

TYPE OF AGENCY—a classification of the agencies covered in this study as (1) departments, (2) agencies, or (3) commissions. (*See* Appendix A for a list of the specific agencies included in each type.)

APPENDIX C

Tables for Chapter 1

TABLE C.1. *Number of Appointments, by Administration and Position Level* [a]

Administration	Appointments		Position Level[b]							
	Number	*Percentage of Total*	Cabinet Secretary	Military Secretary	Under Secretary	Assistant Secretary	General Counsel	Administrator	Deputy Administrator	Commissioner
Roosevelt	365	*23%*	25	—	24	116	19	19	42	120
Truman	401	*26*	28	6	47	139	24	33	37	87
Eisenhower	433	*28*	21	10	55	180	36	22	27	82
Kennedy	212	*14*	13	5	24	100	15	12	9	34
Johnson	156	*10*	12	3	22	78	12	9	8	12
All five	1,567	*100%*[c]	99	24	172	613	106	95	123	335

[a] Includes reappointments.

[b] See Appendix A for the titles of positions included in each level.

[c] Percentages do not add to 100 because of rounding.

TABLE C.2. *Number of Appointments, by Administration and Agency* [a]

		Administration				
Agency	All Five	Roosevelt	Truman	Eisenhower	Kennedy	Johnson
State[b]	182	27	44	56	33	22
Treasury	75	20	14	20	11	10
Defense[c]	81	—	13	40	15	13
Army[d]	68	9	23	18	11	7
Navy	68	13	19	20	7	9
Air Force	51	—	15	20	10	6
Justice	139	45	41	23	15	15
Post Office	70	16	15	20	12	7
Interior	61	13	16	17	7	8
Agriculture	54	14	10	15	9	6
Commerce	81	15	20	23	11	12
Labor	59	12	14	16	10	7
Health, Education, and Welfare[e]	33	3	5	14	6	5
Total departments	1,022	187	249	302	157	127
Agency for International Development[b,f,g]	25	1	11	7	4	2
Bureau of the Budget[g]	28	4	8	11	3	2
Federal Loan Agency[g]	8	7	1	—	—	—
Federal Works Agency[g]	9	5	4	—	—	—
General Services Administration[g]	13	—	1	6	4	2
Housing and Home Finance Agency[g,h]	21	2	8	7	2	2
Veterans Administration[g]	18	2	5	5	2	4
United States Information Agency[g,i]	11	3	—	4	2	2

Depression agencies[j,k]	17	17	—	—	—	—
War and war planning agencies[k,l]	60	17	27	9	4	3
Total agencies	210	58	65	49	21	17
Total departments and agencies	1,232	245	314	351	178	144
Civil Aeronautics Board	41	13	12	12	3	1
Federal Communications Commission	51	22	13	11	5	—
Federal Power Commission	41	15	10	8	7	1
Federal Trade Commission	38	13	10	8	5	2
Interstate Commerce Commission	66	22	16	20	4	4
National Labor Relations Board	35	10	11	9	4	1
Securities and Exchange Commission	63	25	15	14	6	3
Total commissions	335	120	87	82	34	12
Total departments, agencies, and commissions	1,567	365	401	433	212	156

[a] Includes reappointments.

[b] State Department figures do not include the Agency for International Development and its predecessors.

[c] Exclusive of the military departments.

[d] Includes its predecessor, the War Department.

[e] Includes its predecessor, Federal Security Agency.

[f] Includes its predecessors: International Cooperation Administration, Foreign Operations Administration, Technical Cooperation Administration, Mutual Security Agency, Economic Cooperation Administration, Foreign Economic Administration.

[g] For all other text and appendix tables, these appointments (and persons) will be included in "other agencies."

[h] Includes its predecessor, National Housing Agency.

[i] Includes its predecessor, Office of War Information.

[j] Includes Federal Emergency Administration of Public Works, Federal Emergency Relief Administration, National Recovery Administration, Works Progress Administration.

[k] For all other text and appendix tables, these appointments (and persons) will be included in "emergency agencies."

[l] Includes Office of Emergency Planning, Office of Civil and Defense Mobilization, Office of Defense Mobilization, Office of Price Administration, Office of War Mobilization, Office of War Mobilization and Reconversion, War Production Board, Federal Civil Defense Administration, Economic Stabilization Agency, Defense Production Administration.

TABLE C.3. *Number of Appointments Received by Each Person* [a]

| Number of Appointments | Persons | |
	Number	Percentage of Total
One	656	*63%*
Two	274	*26*
Three	86	*8*
Four	20	*2*
Five	5	*1*
Total	1,041	*100*

[a] Includes reappointments.

APPENDIX D

Tables for Chapter 2

TABLE D.1. *Distribution by Census Region of United States Population, 1900 and 1950, and of Sources of Federal Political Executives, 1933–1961* [a]

| Census Region | U. S. Population[b] | | Federal Political Executives | | |
	1900	1950	Birthplace	Legal Residence	Location of Principal Occupation
Pacific	3%	10%	5%	7%	6%
Mountain	2	3	4	6	4
West North Central	14	9	14	8	6
East North Central	21	20	19	16	14
West South Central	9	10	7	6	5
East South Central	10	8	5	3	1
South Atlantic[c]	14	14	12	20	30
Middle Atlantic	20	20	20	24	23
New England	7	6	10	11	6
Foreign and other	—	—	4	—	5[d]
Number of persons	—	—	778	771	779

a These figures include only executives appointed through the "first round" of Kennedy appointments (to the end of 1961), excluding all commissioners. Percentages may not add to 100 because of rounding.

b Source: U.S. Census data.

c Including Washington, D.C.

d This category includes political executives whose principal occupations before appointment had been overseas or in the military service.

TABLE D.2. *Location by Census Region of Principal Occupations Before Appointment, Compared with United States Population (1950 Census), by Administration* [a]

Census Region	1950 Population	All Five	Administration[b]				
			Roosevelt	Truman	Eisenhower	Kennedy	Johnson
Pacific	10%	7%	3%	5%	8%	10%	10%
Mountain	3	3	3	2	4	3	3
West North Central	9	6	4	2	11	4	5
East North Central	20	13	14	7	15	9	8
West South Central	10	5	6	5	4	4	2
East South Central	8	2	3	1	1	2	1
South Atlantic	14	31	33	51	22	34	37
Washington, D. C.	(0.5)	(26)	(28)	(45)	(19)	(31)	(34)
Other South Atlantic	(13.5)	(5)	(5)	(6)	(3)	(3)	(3)
Middle Atlantic	20	20	22	18	22	19	18
New England	6	7	9	4	6	9	9
Foreign and other[c]	...	6	4	5	7	6	8
Number of persons[d]		1,024	264	314	345	191	147

[a] Percentages may not add to 100 because of rounding.

[b] Occupation before the first political executive position, regardless of the administration, is tabulated in the total of all persons. Occupation before the first appointment (or reappointment) in that administration is tabulated in the breakdown by administration.

[c] This category, not matched in the census data, is made up of political executives whose principal occupations before appointment had been overseas or in the military service.

[d] Numbers of persons in individual administrations do not add to the total for all administrations, because a person is counted once in each administration he served, but only once in the total for all five administrations.

111

TABLE D.3. *Location by Census Region of Principal Occupations Before Appointment, by Agency* [a]

Agency[b]	Pacific	Mountain	West North Central	East North Central	West South Central	East South Central	South Atlantic	Middle Atlantic	New England	Foreign and Other	Number of Persons[c]
	7%	3%	6%	13%	5%	2%	31%	20%	7%	6%	
All departments, agencies, and commissions											1,024
State	4	—	2	4	2	1	35	15	5	33	130
Treasury	—	2	6	14	2	—	27	36	13	—	55
Defense	12	—	5	16	3	—	25	31	6	2	64
Army	8	4	8	17	2	2	21	33	4	—	48
Navy	12	5	2	12	10	—	17	26	12	5	42
Air Force	9	—	6	6	6	—	21	50	3	—	34
Justice	9	2	5	8	5	2	36	23	9	—	99
Post Office	5	5	5	21	9	—	29	23	2	—	56
Interior	10	36	14	7	2	7	24	7	—	—	42
Agriculture	12	7	14	7	10	—	38	5	—	—	42
Commerce	10	—	6	15	4	—	25	31	3	6	68
Labor	7	—	2	20	4	2	33	20	11	—	45
HEW	—	—	7	30	4	—	30	18	11	—	27

All departments	8	4	6	12	4	1	29	23	6	7	707
Emergency agencies	2	—	10	21	5	3	36	18	3	3	62
Other agencies	2	1	10	14	7	1	32	20	8	4	99
All agencies	2	1	10	17	6	2	34	19	6	4	158
All departments and agencies	7	3	6	13	4	1	29	23	6	6	835
CAB	11	—	4	7	7	—	37	15	11	7	27
FCC	6	3	3	12	3	9	50	6	6	6	34
FPC	20	8	4	8	16	4	20	8	12	—	25
FTC	—	—	12	4	—	—	69	8	8	—	26
ICC	6	9	9	12	9	9	33	3	9	—	33
NLRB	8	—	4	8	4	—	48	20	8	—	25
SEC	7	2	2	10	2	2	32	24	17	—	41
All commissions	8	3	5	9	6	4	41	13	10	2	207

113

a Percentages may not add to 100 because of rounding.

b Occupation before the first federal political executive position, regardless of the agency, is tabulated in the total of all departments, agencies, and commissions. Occupation before the first appointment in that agency or agency grouping is tabulated in the breakdown by agency or agency grouping.

c Numbers of persons in individual agency groupings (for example, State, Emergency agencies) do not add to the subtotals (All departments, All commissions) or the total departments, agencies, and commissions, because a person is counted once in each agency grouping in which he served, but only once in a subtotal or total grouping.

TABLE D.4. *Size of Community of Principal Occupations Before Appointment, by Administration, Compared with United States Population (1950 Census)* ᵃ

Size of Communityᵇ	U. S. Population	Administration					
		All Five	Roosevelt	Truman	Eisenhower	Kennedy	Johnson
Under 25,000	59%	11%	10%	8%	14%	9%	7%
25,000 to 99,999	12	11	16	5	8	14	16
100,000 to 399,999	10	14	12	11	17	13	13
400,000 and up (except Washington and New York City)	14	21	15	14	26	19	14
Washington, D. C.	0.5	28	30	47	20	34	37
New York City	5	14	17	15	14	12	12
Number of personsᶜ	d	952	246	298	319	175	134

ᵃ Percentages may not add to 100 because of rounding.

ᵇ Occupation before the first political executive position, regardless of the administration, is tabulated in the total of all persons. Occupation before the first appointment (or reappointment) in that administration is tabulated in the breakdown by administration.

ᶜ Numbers of persons in individual administrations do not add to the total for all administrations, because a person is counted once in each administration he served, but only once in the total for all five administrations.

ᵈ Approximately 151 million.

115

TABLE D.5. Size of Community of Principal Occupations Before Appointment, by Agency [a]

	Size of Community						
Agency[b]	Under 25,000	25,000–99,999	100,000–399,999	400,000 and up (except Washington and New York City)	Washington, D. C.	New York City	Number of Persons[c]
All departments, agencies, and commissions	11%	11%	14%	21%	28%	14%	952
State	4	5	13	10	50	19	86
Treasury	7	9	11	20	20	32	54
Defense	13	10	6	32	22	18	63
Army	8	13	26	8	11	34	47
Navy	12	15	15	30	12	15	40
Air Force	15	6	12	18	18	32	34
Justice	8	9	9	33	26	15	98
Post Office	13	11	18	26	26	7	55
Interior	34	17	12	7	24	5	41
Agriculture	25	20	12	8	32	2	40
Commerce	12	8	14	27	20	19	64
Labor	9	7	18	29	29	9	45
HEW	15	11	15	22	26	11	27

All departments	12	11	14	22	26	17	651
Emergency agencies	14	14	5	22	33	12	58
Other agencies	10	4	17	21	32	17	95
All agencies	11	8	13	21	32	15	150
All departments and agencies	12	10	14	22	26	16	772
CAB	17	17	12	17	29	8	24
FCC	3	19	12	12	47	6	32
FPC	17	25	29	12	17	–	24
FTC	8	12	4	4	68	4	25
ICC	19	19	28	12	22	–	32
NLRB	16	4	12	20	44	4	25
SEC	2	5	15	25	32	20	40
All commissions	11	13	16	16	37	7	198

ᵃ Percentages may not add to 100 because of rounding.

ᵇ Occupation before the first federal political executive position, regardless of the agency, is tabulated in the total of all departments, agencies, and commissions. Occupation before the first appointment in that agency or agency grouping is tabulated in the breakdown by agency or agency grouping.

ᶜ Numbers of persons in individual agency groupings (for example, State, Emergency agencies) do not add to the subtotals (All departments, All commissions) or the total departments, agencies, and commissions, because a person is counted once in each agency grouping in which he served, but only once in a subtotal or total grouping.

TABLE D.6. *Level of Education, by Position Level* [a]

Position Level	Undergraduate			Graduate [b]				Number of Persons [c]
	No College	*Some College No Degree*	*College Graduate*	*Some Graduate Work No Degree*	*Primary Law Degree*	*Master's Degree*	*Doctorate* [d]	
All levels	7%	17%	76%	17%	44%	17%	11%	1,026
Cabinet secretary	8	22	70	12	46	11	5	82
Military secretary	17	4	78	26	52	4	—	23
Under secretary	6	15	79	15	33	17	11	148
Assistant secretary	7	16	77	19	38	20	13	485
General counsel	7	10	83	13	96	10	5	83
Administrator	6	20	74	27	27	20	10	77
Deputy administrator	9	19	72	15	30	18	11	99
Commissioner	7	19	74	7	59	13	6	207

[a] Percentages may not add to 100 because of rounding.

[b] Categories of graduate degrees are not mutually exclusive. A person is counted once for each type of degree he holds.

[c] Numbers of persons in individual position levels do not add to the total for all levels, because a person is counted once in each position level in which he served, but only once in the total for all levels.

[d] Does not include honorary degrees or primary law degrees.

119

TABLE D.7. *Level of Education, by Agency* [a]

| Agency | *No College* | Undergraduate | | Graduate[b] | | | | *Number of Persons*[c] |
		Some College No Degree	*College Graduate*	*Some Graduate Work No Degree*	*Primary Law Degree*	*Master's Degree*	*Doctorate*[d]	
All departments, agencies, and commissions	7%	17%	76%	17%	44%	17%	11%	1,026
State	3	14	83	35	27	25	11	180
Treasury	2	11	87	6	46	19	15	54
Defense	8	8	84	13	40	14	14	63
Army	6	4	90	19	52	15	4	48
Navy	12	17	71	12	41	19	5	42
Air Force	3	6	91	20	43	20	17	35
Justice	6	15	79	15	84	10	10	99
Post Office	12	38	50	4	39	7	2	56
Interior	5	21	74	17	45	17	10	42
Agriculture	2	26	71	17	29	29	29	42
Commerce	9	16	75	12	27	16	12	67
Labor	21	11	68	26	32	15	13	47
HEW	7	7	85	26	48	26	11	27

120

All departments	7	16	77	18	42	18	12	708
Emergency agencies	5	25	70	16	27	18	14	63
Other agencies	7	17	76	25	29	20	9	98
All agencies	6	20	73	22	28	20	11	158
All departments and agencies	7	16	77	19	40	18	12	837
CAB	4	22	74	7	56	15	15	27
FCC	9	24	68	—	53	6	3	34
FPC	12	28	60	12	44	16	4	25
FTC	12	12	77	8	77	12	4	26
ICC	3	21	76	3	64	12	6	33
NLRB	—	16	84	12	48	20	12	25
SEC	7	12	80	10	63	12	5	41
All commissions	7	19	74	7	59	13	6	207

121

Table D.8. *Type of Precollege Education, by Administration* [a]

| Administration | Number of Persons[b] | | | Private[c] | | | Public Only[c] | Uncertain[c] |
	Total	No Data	Data Available	Best-Known Preparatory[d]	Other Private	Total Private[e]		
All five	1,041	491	550	17%	26%	39%	59%	2%
Roosevelt	277	165	112	15	33	40	57	3
Truman	318	135	188	14	26	37	61	2
Eisenhower	347	153	194	19	28	43	57	1
Kennedy	191	80	111	19	18	35	61	4
Johnson	147	66	81	18	20	37	56	7

[a] Percentages may not add to 100 because of rounding.

[b] Numbers of persons in individual administrations do not add to the total for all administrations, because a person is counted once in each administration he served, but only once in the total for all five administrations.

[c] Percentages of federal executives in these categories are based on figures in "Data Available" column.

[d] See listing in text, pp. 20-21.

[e] "Total private" may not be the sum of the previous two columns because some persons have attended both the best-known preparatory and other private schools. They are then counted once in each type but only once in the "Total private" category.

TABLE D.9. *Type of Precollege Education, by Agency* [a]

Agency	Number of Persons[b]			Private[c]			Public Only[e]	Uncertain[e]
	Total	No Data	Data Available	Best-Known Preparatory[d]	Other Private	Total Private[e]		
All departments, agencies, and commissions	1,041	491	550	17%	26%	39%	59%	2%
State	131	57	74	38	27	60	38	3
Treasury	55	29	26	31	23	46	54	—
Defense	64	30	34	26	18	44	53	3
Army	48	22	26	31	27	54	46	—
Navy	42	16	26	35	31	54	46	—
Air Force	35	21	14	14	29	43	50	7
Justice	99	50	49	16	26	39	59	2
Post Office	56	21	35	6	29	34	66	—
Interior	42	25	17	—	12	12	88	—
Agriculture	42	21	21	—	10	10	90	—
Commerce	68	33	35	17	20	34	51	14
Labor	48	17	31	6	39	39	55	6
HEW	27	15	12	8	42	50	50	—

All departments	712	340	372	20	26	42	56	3
Emergency agencies	70	41	29	10	34	38	59	3
Other agencies	102	54	48	21	27	42	54	4
All agencies	169	93	76	17	30	41	55	4
All departments and agencies	851	420	431	19	27	42	56	3
CAB	27	14	13	23	54	54	46	—
FCC	35	11	24	8	25	29	67	4
FPC	25	5	20	—	—	—	95	5
FTC	26	10	16	12	38	44	56	—
ICC	33	11	22	—	18	18	82	—
NLRB	25	11	14	—	21	21	79	—
SEC	41	19	22	18	36	50	50	—
All commissions	208	80	128	9	25	29	70	1

a Percentages may not add to 100 because of rounding.

b Numbers of persons in individual agency groupings (for example, State, Emergency agencies) do not add to the subtotals (All departments, All commissions) or the total departments, agencies, and commissions, because a person is counted once in each agency grouping in which he served, but only once in a subtotal or total grouping.

c Percentages of federal executives in these categories are based on figures in "Data Available" column.

d See listing in text, pp. 20-21.

e "Total private" may not be the sum of the previous two columns because some persons have attended both the best-known preparatory and other private schools. They are then counted once in each type but only once in the "total private" category.

TABLE D.10. *Undergraduate Universities and Colleges Attended by Largest Percentage of Federal Political Executives, by Administration* [a]

		Administration					
Rank	School	All Five	Roosevelt	Truman	Eisenhower	Kennedy	Johnson
1	Yale	7.8%	6.7%	8.8%	7.2%	9.4%	10.2%
2	Harvard	6.4	6.3	4.1	7.8	6.3	8.2
3	Princeton	5.2	2.6	5.0	7.2	5.8	6.8
4	Wisconsin	2.1	3.7	1.9	2.3	2.1	1.4
5	Dartmouth	1.9	2.2	1.6	3.7	1.0	1.4
6	California (Berkeley)	1.8	0.7	0.9	3.2	1.6	1.4
7	Michigan	1.7	0.7	1.3	2.3	2.1	3.4
8	Stanford	1.6	0.7	1.3	2.3	1.0	1.4
9.5	Chicago	1.5	2.6	1.9	—	2.1	1.4
9.5	North Carolina	1.5	1.9	2.2	0.3	2.1	2.0
11	Minnesota	1.4	0.4	0.6	2.0	2.1	1.4
12	Nebraska	1.2	1.9	0.9	1.4	0.5	0.7
14	Columbia	1.1	0.7	1.3	1.2	1.6	1.4
14	Cornell	1.1	0.7	—	2.0	1.0	1.4
14	Northwestern	1.1	0.4	0.9	0.9	2.6	0.7
17	Kentucky	1.0	0.7	1.3	0.9	1.0	0.7
17	Texas	1.0	1.5	1.3	0.9	1.6	1.4
17	U.S. Military Academy	1.0	1.1	1.3	1.2	0.5	—
	Top eighteen	40.2	35.7	36.6	46.7	44.5	44.9
	Ivy League	25.1	20.8	22.1	31.1	26.2	29.2
	"Big Three"	19.5	15.6	18.0	22.2	21.5	25.2
Number of persons[b]		1,032	269	317	347	191	147

[a] Only one undergraduate college was coded for each person: the school at which the bachelor's degree (other than a law degree) was obtained or the last school attended if no undergraduate or graduate degree was obtained.

[b] Numbers of persons in individual administrations do not add to the total for all administrations, because a person is counted once in each administration he served, but only once in the total for all five administrations.

126

TABLE D.11. *Rankings of Leading Undergraduate Universities and Colleges Attended by Federal Political Executives and Big Business Executives*

Institution	Federal Political Executives[a]	Big Business Executives	
		Newcomer[b] (1950)	Scientific American[c] (1964)
Yale	1	2	1
Harvard	2	1	2
Princeton	3	3	3
Wisconsin	4	8	9.5
Dartmouth	5	d	9.5
California (Berkeley)	6	10[e]	11.5[e]
Michigan	7	5	13
Stanford	8	d	7
Chicago	9.5	d	23
North Carolina	9.5	d	f
Cornell	14	4	6
Columbia	14	6	15
Pennsylvania	19	9	8
M. I. T.	21.5	7	4
Illinois	21.5	d	5
New York University	37.5	d	18

[a] From Table D.10 above, p. 126.
[b] Mabel Newcomer, *The Big Business Executive* (Columbia University Press, 1955), p. 74.
[c] *The Big Business Executive/1964* (Scientific American, 1965), p. 41.
[d] Not listed: only ten institutions ranked.
[e] Entire University of California—Berkeley not tabulated separately.
[f] Fewer than three persons attended, so not ranked.

TABLE D.12. *Graduate Schools Attended by Largest Percentage of Federal Political Executives*

Rank	School	All Persons with Graduate Work	Persons with Law Degrees	Persons with Graduate Work, No Degree	Persons with Graduate Degrees, but No Law Degree
1	[Harvard Law]	15.4%	21.9%	7.0%	2.9%
	[Harvard—other than law]	6.8	2.3	9.3	17.3
2	Yale	8.1	10.6	2.3	4.6
3	Columbia	7.3	5.4	5.8	12.7
4	George Washington	5.1	6.8	5.8	0.6
5	Oxford	5.0	3.2	9.3	7.5
6	Michigan	4.7	4.1	1.2	8.1
7	Chicago	4.0	1.8	5.8	8.7
8	Georgetown	3.1	4.3	2.3	0.6
9	California (Berkeley)	2.4	0.9	1.2	6.9
10	Wisconsin	2.3	0.7	3.5	5.8
11	Texas	2.1	2.7	1.2	1.2
12	Cornell	2.0	1.4	3.5	2.9
13	Virginia	1.9	2.3	1.2	1.2
16	Fordham	1.6	2.5	—	—
16	Minnesota	1.6	1.4	—	2.9
16	Northwestern	1.6	1.4	2.3	1.7
16	Princeton	1.6	0.9	—	4.0
16	Stanford	1.6	1.4	1.2	2.3
Number of persons[a]		701	442	86	173

[a] The percentage base in this table is the number of persons who have done graduate work or a specific type of graduate work. Only two graduate schools were coded for any person and an attempt was made to select the most significant ones (usually those where degrees were obtained) if a person attended more than two.

TABLE D.13. *Distribution and Medians of Ages at Appointment, by Position Level* [a]

| | Age at Appointment | | | | | |
Position Level[b]	30's or Under	40's	50's	60's and Over	Median Age	Number of Persons[c]
All levels	17%	41%	30%	12%	48	1,010
Cabinet secretary	2	31	40	26	53	83
Military secretary	4	26	48	22	54	23
Under secretary	4	46	35	16	50	146
Assistant secretary	18	44	28	10	46	482
General counsel	29	39	17	15	44	82
Administrator	5	35	47	13	51	75
Deputy administrator	20	38	31	11	47	93
Commissioner	18	41	29	12	48	204

[a] Percentages may not add to 100 because of rounding.

[b] In the distributions by position level, age at the time of first appointment to that level is tabulated. In the distribution for all levels, age at the time of first appointment, regardless of the position level, is tabulated.

[c] Numbers of persons in individual position levels do not add to the total for all levels, because a person is counted once in each position level in which he served, but only once in the total for all levels.

129

TABLE D.14. *Median Age at Appointment, by Administration and Position Level* [a]

				Position Level						
Administration	All Levels	Cabinet Secretary	Military Secretary	Under Secretary	Assistant Secretary	General Counsel	Administrator	Deputy Administrator	Commissioner	Number of Persons[b]
All five	48	53	54	50	46	44	51	47	48	1,010
Roosevelt	49	53	—	49	48	38	51	47	50	256
Truman	46	53	51	50	43	41	52	44	53	310
Eisenhower	51	54	58	53	51	48	52	51	49	345
Kennedy	47	50	45	48	47	44	50	43	47	191
Johnson	48	52	53	48	46	52	47	47	54	144

[a] For the breaks by administration, age at the time of first appointment to a position level in an administration is counted. For all administrations, age at the time of first appointment, regardless of the position level, is tabulated.

[b] Numbers of persons in individual position levels do not add to the total for all levels, because a person is counted once in each position level in which he served, but only once in the total for all levels.

130

APPENDIX E

Tables for Chapter 3

TABLE E.1. *Principal Occupations Before Appointment, by Administration* [a]

Occupation	Administration[b]					
	All Five	Roosevelt	Truman	Eisenhower	Kennedy	Johnson
Business	24%	20%	20%	34%	17%	20%
Law	26	24	22	26	25	20
Education	7	10	2	5	12	11
Science or engineering	2	2	1	1	4	3
Other private	6	6	4	5	9	9
Total private	64	62	48	71	67	63
Public service, elective	4	5	4	4	3	3
Appointive (federal)	22	23	41	18	22	20
Appointive (nonfederal)	9	9	7	7	8	13
Total government	36	38	52	29	33	37
Number of persons[c]	1,082	269	317	347	191	147

[a] Percentages may not add to 100 or subtotals because of rounding.
[b] Occupation before the first political executive position, regardless of the administration, is tabulated in the "All five" column. Occupation before the first appointment (or reappointment) in a specific administration is tabulated in the breakdown by administration.
[c] Numbers of persons in individual administrations do not add to the total for all administrations, because a person is counted once in each administration he served, but only once in the total for all five administrations.

TABLE E.2. *Secondary Occupations, by Administration* ᵃ

			Administrationᵇ			
Occupation	All Five	Roosevelt	Truman	Eisenhower	Kennedy	Johnson
No secondary occupation	42%	44%	31%	44%	40%	44%
Business	12	9	12	16	10	4
Law	14	15	21	12	12	13
Education	5	2	5	5	6	6
Science or engineering	2	1	1	2	2	2
Other private	4	3	4	2	3	3
Total private	36	31	43	37	32	28
Public service, elective	2	3	2	3	4	5
Appointive (federal)	13	13	18	10	16	18
Appointive (nonfederal)	7	10	5	7	7	5
Total government	22	25	25	19	27	28
Number of personsᶜ	1,083	270	317	347	191	147

ᵃ Percentages may not add to 100 or subtotals because of rounding.
ᵇ Occupation before the first political executive position, regardless of the administration, is tabulated in the "All five" column. Occupation before the first appointment (or reappointment) in a specific administration is tabulated in the breakdown by administration.
ᶜ Numbers of persons in individual administrations do not add to the total for all administrations, because a person is counted once in each administration he served, but only once in the total for all five administrations.

133

TABLE E.3. *Principal Occupations Before Appointment, by Agency* [a]

Agency[b]	Private						Public				Number of Persons[c]
	Business	Law	Education	Science or Engineering	Other	Total Private	Elective	Appointive (Federal)	Appointive (Non-federal)	Total Public	
All departments, agencies, and commissions	24%	26%	7%	2%	6%	64%	4%	22%	9%	36%	1,032
State	16	10	8	2	5	40	5	51	4	60	131
Treasury	44	34	4	2	—	84	—	13	4	16	55
Defense	39	25	9	5	9	88	—	12	—	12	64
Army	40	40	4	2	—	85	2	2	10	15	48
Navy	60	24	2	2	2	91	2	7	—	10	42
Air Force	34	31	11	6	—	83	2	17	—	17	35
Justice	1	64	7	—	—	72	2	22	4	28	99
Post Office	34	21	2	2	7	66	—	23	11	34	56
Interior	26	26	5	—	5	62	5	24	10	38	42
Agriculture	14	10	19	—	19	62	5	19	14	38	42
Commerce	57	19	6	3	2	87	2	10	2	13	68
Labor	12	17	10	—	31	71	2	12	15	29	48
HEW	22	22	18	—	4	67	4	22	7	33	27

134

All departments	27	27	8	2	6	70	2	22	6	30	712
Emergency agencies	33	16	5	3	10	67	6	21	6	33	63
Other agencies	33	11	6	2	10	62	2	26	10	38	100
All agencies	32	13	6	2	10	64	4	24	8	36	160
All departments and agencies	28	25	7	2	7	69	3	22	6	31	842
CAB	15	33	11	4	4	67	4	18	11	33	27
FCC	6	29	—	—	3	37	17	34	11	63	35
FPC	8	28	—	—	8	44	8	8	40	56	25
FTC	4	27	4	3	—	35	23	38	4	65	26
ICC	12	36	3	—	—	54	3	9	33	46	33
NLRB	20	16	12	—	—	48	8	20	24	52	25
SEC	17	24	7	—	—	49	7	24	20	51	41
All commissions	12	28	4	1	2	47	10	23	20	53	208

a Percentages may not add to subtotals or 100 because of rounding.

b Occupation before the first federal political executive position, regardless of the agency, is tabulated in the total of all departments, agencies, and commissions. Occupation before the first appointment in that agency or agency grouping is tabulated in the breakdown by agency or agency grouping.

c Number of persons in individual agency groupings (for example, State, Emergency agencies) do not add to the subtotals (All commissions, All departments, All commissions) or the total departments, agencies, and commissions, because a person is counted once in each agency grouping in which he served, but only once in a subtotal or total grouping.

135

TABLE E.4. *Commissioners Who Worked in a Commission-Related Industry or Function Before Appointment, by Administration and Agency* [a]

Administration	Commission							
	All Seven	*CAB*	*FCC*	*FPC*	*FTC*	*ICC*	*NLRB*	*SEC*
All five[b]	17%	19%	14%	12%	4%	21%	8%	34%
Roosevelt	11	11	12	—	—	38	—	13
Truman	28	44	38	—	—	25	33	33
Eisenhower	20	—	14	14	17	17	—	67
Kennedy	12	—	—	33	—	—	—	25
Johnson	29	c	c	c	—	—	—	67
Number of persons[c]	212	27	35	25	26	33	25	41

_a Example of how this table is to be read and interpreted: Of the commissioners appointed by President Truman to the ICC, 25 percent had been employed in, or retained by, industries or functions primarily concerned with surface transportation within two years before their/appointments to that commission, or to other government positions preceding such appointment.

_b A commissioner is counted only under the President who first appointed him to that commission. Nine persons whose first appointments were pre-Roosevelt (and who were reappointed by Roosevelt) are not included in the administration breaks but are included in the totals.

_c There were no Johnson appointees in these commissions before April 30, 1965.

136

TABLE E.5. *Types of Federal Positions Previously Held by Appointees, by Administration*

Adminis-tration	Federal Political Executive		Other Noncareer		Career		Con-gress	Judi-cial	Part-Time	Political Party	No Federal Service	Number of Appoint-ments[a]
	Same Agency	Other Agen-cies	Same Agency	Other Agen-cies	Same Agency	Other Agen-cies						
All five	29%	11%	24%	37%	14%	11%	6%	1%	18%	7%	15%	1,558
Roosevelt	25	11	21	41	10	8	7	2	15	7	17	358
Truman	32	13	30	41	16	14	5	2	17	4	10	399
Eisenhower	19	10	22	25	13	8	7	b	17	7	24	433
Kennedy	16	9	23	45	17	14	4	—	24	11	13	212
Johnson	73	9	29	42	15	15	5	—	21	8	2	156

a Includes reappointments.
b Less than 0.5 percent.

137

TABLE E.6. *Types of Federal Positions Previously Held by Appointees, by Position Level*

Position Level	Federal Political Executive		Other Noncareer		Career		Con-gress	Judi-cial	Part-Time	Political Party	No Federal Service	Number of Appoint-ments[a]
	Same Agency	Other Agen-cies	Same Agency	Other Agen-cies	Same Agency	Other Agen-cies						
All levels	29%	11%	24%	37%	14%	11%	6%	1%	18%	7%	15%	1,558
Cabinet secretary	40	29	17	38	2	3	16	6	24	15	12	99
Military secretary	50	38	25	54	—	—	—	—	33	17	4	24
Under secretary	44	18	22	36	9	11	5	1	22	13	9	172
Assistant secretary	20	5	36	31	19	10	3	b	19	5	17	612
General counsel	20	5	35	47	15	8	6	—	10	6	17	106
Administrator	21	20	16	46	5	16	7	3	21	11	15	95
Deputy administrator	11	9	20	46	18	27	1	—	14	4	15	115
Commissioner	42	11	8	39	11	11	11	b	14	4	15	385

a Includes reappointments.
b Less than 0.5 percent.

139

TABLE E.7. Types of Federal Positions Previously Held by Appointees, by Agency

Agency	Federal Political Executive		Other Noncareer		Career		Con-gress	Judi-cial	Part-Time	Political Party	No Federal Service	Number of Appoint-ments[a]
	Same Agency	Other Agen-cies	Same Agency	Other Agen-cies	Same Agency	Other Agen-cies						
All departments, agencies, and commissions	29%	11%	24%	37%	14%	11%	6%	1%	18%	7%	15%	1,558
State	30	13	39	40	41	13	5	1	16	3	6	181
Treasury	27	15	36	37	12	8	3	1	20	8	12	75
Defense	22	22	32	33	—	14	3	—	32	9	17	81
Army	32	6	25	21	—	3	2	4	29	3	20	68
Navy	37	12	21	37	7	6	2	—	15	10	22	68
Air Force	33	6	29	35	14	10	—	—	18	8	16	51
Justice	29	4	49	37	8	4	3	3	7	7	16	139
Post Office	19	1	17	33	17	3	4	—	13	27	18	70
Interior	31	11	10	31	18	25	15	—	16	5	18	61
Agriculture	22	2	41	20	28	2	6	—	28	6	15	54
Commerce	17	19	22	32	3	11	7	—	27	11	17	81
Labor	19	10	27	36	3	9	3	2	29	—	17	59
HEW	18	15	18	55	9	6	12	—	21	15	15	33

All departments	27	10	31	35	15	9	5	1	19	8	15	1,021
Emergency agencies	9	14	20	47	7	19	6	3	17	7	13	70
Other agencies	21	14	17	46	15	24	3	1	17	7	16	132
All agencies	17	14	18	46	12	22	4	2	17	7	15	202
All departments and agencies	25	11	29	37	14	11	4	1	19	8	15	1,223
CAB	34	32	2	56	2	5	24	—	24	—	12	41
FCC	33	12	12	41	22	28	6	2	10	12	8	51
FPC	49	2	2	37	2	10	5	—	10	—	22	41
FTC	42	3	3	45	11	18	26	—	11	11	5	38
ICC	65	12	5	23	8	5	3	—	11	—	20	66
NLRB	29	6	20	37	6	11	14	—	17	—	11	35
SEC	35	6	11	44	21	5	6	—	18	3	19	63
All commissions	42	10	8	39	11	11	11	b	14	4	15	335

a Includes reappointments.
b Less than 0.5 percent.

TABLE E.8. *Distribution by Administration of Percentages and Median Years of Service of Federal Political Executives with Prior Federal Administrative Service in the Same Agency, and in Other Agencies*

| Administration[a] | Service in Same Agency | | Service in Other Agencies | | Average Number of Persons[c] |
	Percentage	Median Service[b] (Years)	Percentage	Median Service[b] (Years)	
All five	35%	4.3	43%	4.1	1,030
Roosevelt	38	4.9	42	3.5	269
Truman	52	5.5	53	5.2	316
Eisenhower	34	4.5	33	4.0	346
Kennedy	39	4.1	54	4.2	191
Johnson	85	4.0	52	4.2	147

[a] In the figures for all five administrations, prior service in the agency of the first political executive appointment (regardless of the President making the appointment) is counted as "same agency service." In the breaks by administration, prior service in the agency of the first appointment by that President is counted as "same agency service."

[b] Grouped median of those with some prior federal administration service.

[c] Numbers of persons in individual administrations do not add to the total for all administrations, because a person is counted once in each administration he served, but only once in the total for all five administrations.

TABLE E.9. *Distribution of Total Years of Federal Administrative Service Before Appointment, by Position Level*[a]

Position Level[b]	No Service	Years of Service					Median of Those with Service[c] (Years)	Number of Persons[d]
		1-2	3-5	6-10	11-15	16 and Over		
All levels	37%	18%	14%	11%	7%	11%	5.2	1,027
Cabinet secretary	37	6	21	24	6	5	6.4	84
Military secretary	9	35	39	9	9	—	3.3	23
Under secretary	22	26	22	13	5	12	4.3	149
Assistant secretary	31	20	17	10	9	13	5.1	486
General counsel	32	22	13	17	7	8	5.2	88
Administrator	28	16	20	19	6	11	5.5	80
Deputy administrator	22	19	15	14	13	15	7.0	98
Commissioner	43	16	10	14	9	8	6.6	205

[a] Percentages may not add to 100 because of rounding.

[b] In the groupings by position level, service before the first appointment at that level is tabulated. In the distribution for all position levels, service before the first political executive appointment, regardless of position level, is tabulated.

[c] Grouped medians.

[d] Numbers of persons in individual position levels do not add to the total for all levels, because a person is counted once in each position level in which he served, but only once in the total for all levels.

143

TABLE E.10. *Types of Prior Nonfederal Public Service* [a]

Type of Public Service	All Federal Political Executives	Federal Political Executives in Departments and Agencies	Commissioners
No nonfederal prior service	62%	63%	55%
State governors	3	3	2
Members of state legislature	7	7	9
Other state officials	3	2	5
Local elected officials	6	6	9
Other local officials	17	13	33
State and local judiciary	3	2	7
Part-time state and local officials	14	14	16
International organization officials (full-time)	1	1	—
International organization officials (part-time)	1	1	1
State and local political party officers	10	10	6
Number of persons[b]	1,031	842	207

[a] Percentages add to more than 100 because some persons served in more than one type of position.

[b] Numbers of persons in columns headed "commissioners" and "federal political executives in departments and agencies" do not add to "all federal political executives" because some persons have held both types of appointment and are counted once in each category but only once in the total.

144

TABLE E.11. *Distribution of Years of Government Administrative Service Before Appointment, by Administration* [a]

Administration [b]		No Service	Years of Service					Median of Those with Service [c] (Years)	Number of Persons [d]
			1–2	3–5	6–10	11–15	16 and Over		
All five:	Total	27%	17%	17%	16%	9%	14%	6.1	1,029
	Commissioners	22	10	20	22	11	14	7.4	207
	Others	28	19	17	14	9	14	5.5	840
Roosevelt:	Total	22	21	16	21	5	16	6.2	269
	Commissioners	20	11	12	33	7	17	8.1	75
	Others	22	25	17	18	4	14	5.0	202
Truman:	Total	16	9	20	19	18	17	8.9	316
	Commissioners	19	1	18	15	21	25	12.0	67
	Others	15	12	21	19	18	15	8.1	252
Eisenhower:	Total	33	17	17	13	6	13	5.4	345
	Commissioners	13	15	22	27	10	13	6.8	60
	Others	36	18	17	10	6	13	5.0	289
Kennedy:	Total	24	20	13	13	10	19	7.1	191
	Commissioners	20	13	10	17	13	27	10.5	30
	Others	24	22	14	13	10	18	6.6	162
Johnson:	Total	6	11	31	18	13	20	6.8	147
	Commissioners	17	—	17	33	33	—	9.3	12
	Others	5	12	33	17	11	22	6.4	135

[a] Percentages may not add to 100 because of rounding.

[b] Breaks by administration count service before the first appointment in that administration, the first appointment as a commissioner in that administration, and the first federal political executive appointment (other than a commission appointment) in that administration, respectively.

[c] Grouped medians.

[d] Numbers of persons in individual administrations do not add to the total for all administrations, because a person is counted once in each administration he served, but only once in the total for all five administrations. Similarly, numbers of persons in "commissioners" and "others" groupings within an administration do not add to individual administration totals, because a person who has been both a commissioner and another type of federal political executive is counted once in each type but only once in the total.

145

TABLE E.12. *Categories of Positions Held Immediately Before Appointment, by Position Level* [a]

					Position Level					
Category of Position	All Levels	Cabinet Secretary	Military Secretary	Under Secretary	Assistant Secretary	General Counsel	Administrator	Deputy Administrator	Total Other than Commissioner	Commissioner
Business	18%	15%	21%	19%	15%	1%	17%	14%	14%	6%
Law	11	12	12	11	10	31	4	4	11	12
Other private	6	3	4	5	9	4	7	7	7	4
Total private	30	30	38	35	34	36	28	25	33	21
Federal political executive	32	44	62	48	22	20	34	16	28	44
Other federal noncareer appointive	22	5	—	10	29	35	24	40	25	13
Federal career	7	1	—	1	9	6	1	14	7	8
Elective, federal, state, local	4	13	—	2	2	2	6	1	3	6
Other	5	6	—	3	4	2	6	4	4	8
Total government	69	70	62	65	66	64	72	75	67	78
Retired	0.2	—	—	—	0.3	—	—	—	0.2	0.3
Number of appointments[b]	1,556	99	24	171	611	106	95	115	1,221	335

a Percentages may not add to subtotals or 100 because of rounding.
b Includes reappointments.

146

APPENDIX F

Tables for Chapter 4

TABLE F.1. *Distribution of Months of Position Tenure, by Position Level* [a]

Position Level	Position Tenure (Months)										Number of Persons in Position [b]
	0-6	7-12	13-24	25-36	37-48	49-60	61-72	73-84	85-96	97 and Over	
All levels	6%	11%	27%	19%	12%	9%	4%	3%	2%	5%	1,105
All levels except commissioner	7	12	30	20	13	9	3	3	2	1	933
Cabinet secretary	3	9	22	12	18	15	6	4	6	5	78
Military secretary	—	9	41	41	—	4	4	—	—	—	22
Under secretary	10	15	34	19	13	6	1	1	1	1	146
Assistant secretary	7	11	29	21	14	9	3	3	2	1	468
General counsel	1	13	36	15	6	12	4	5	4	4	78
Administrator	7	16	26	25	10	6	7	1	1	1	73
Deputy administrator	15	13	37	13	10	6	2	2	2	2	68
Commissioner	3	5	9	17	10	13	9	8	4	23	172

[a] Percentages may not add to 100 because of rounding.
[b] See Appendix A for an explanation of differences in coverage between tables presenting position tenure only and those which compare position tenure with agency and government tenure.

TABLE F.2. *Medians of Position Tenure, Agency Tenure, and Government Tenure, by Agency* [a]

Agency	Tenure Median (Months)		
	Position	Agency	Government
All departments, agencies, and commissions	28	32	37
State	23	26	28
Treasury	30	32	37
Defense	21	24	26
Army	21	29	36
Navy	25	38	42
Air Force	25	29	32
Justice	29	37	37
Post Office	32	35	36
Interior	38	41	41
Agriculture	30	34	36
Commerce	21	22	24
Labor	31	33	35
HEW	29	31	31
All departments	25	30	34
Emergency agencies	17	18	22
Other agencies	23	27	31
All agencies	21	23	28
All departments and agencies	24	29	34

[a] See explanation in Appendix A concerning coverage of tenure tables and computation of tenure and medians.

TABLE F.3. *Median Months of Position Tenure, by Agency and Position Level* [a]

Agency	All Levels	Position Level						
		Cabinet Secretary	Military Secretary	Under Secretary	Assistant Secretary	General Counsel	Administrator	Deputy Administrator
All departments, agencies, and commissions	27	39	24	20	26	25	25	21
State	23	24	—	15	23	33	—	—
Treasury	29	51	—	30	30	21	—	—
Defense	20	18	18	16	23	16	—	—
Army	21	41	21	17	21	21	—	—
Navy	26	38	31	19	30	5[b]	—	—
Air Force	25	—	—	26	22	27	—	—
Justice	27	41	—	24	27	—	—	—
Post Office	31	59	—	23	30	49	—	—
Interior	39	45	—	23	41	24	—	—
Agriculture	30	58	—	30	24	55	—	—
Commerce	22	35	—	20	24	21	—	—
Labor	29	44	—	20	30	25	—	—
HEW	29	31	—	18	31	93[b]	65[c,d]	24[d]
Emergency agencies	15	—	—	—	—	—	16	15
Other agencies	24	—	—	—	—	—	29	22

[a] See explanation in Appendix A concerning coverage of tenure tables and computation of tenure and medians.
[b] Number (1 unit is one person in one position in an agency) is only 1.
[c] Number (1 unit is one person in one position in an agency) is only 3.
[d] In the Federal Security Agency, a predecessor of the Department of Health, Education, and Welfare.

TABLE F.4. *Percentages of Federal Political Executives with Two Years or Less, over Three Years, and over Four Years of Position Tenure, Ranked by Agency* [a]

Two Years or Less		Over Three Years (Inverse Ranking)		Over Four Years (Inverse Ranking)	
Defense	63%	Defense	17%	Navy	4%
Army	60	Commerce	21	Defense	11
Commerce	59	Air Force	23	State	12
State	55	Army	25	Commerce	15
Air Force	49	Navy	25	Army	15
All departments	48	State	28	Air Force	18
Navy	48	*All departments*	32	*All departments*	19
Treasury	43	HEW	32	Justice	21
Justice	42	Justice	37	HEW	24
Labor	41	Agriculture	38	Interior	25
Agriculture	38	Treasury	41	Treasury	25
Post Office	36	Labor	41	Labor	27
Interior	36	Post Office	42	Agriculture	31
HEW	36	Interior	52	Post Office	34
Emergency agencies	68	Emergency agencies	15	Emergency agencies	7
All agencies	58	*All agencies*	23	*All agencies*	13
Other agencies	53	Other agencies	27	Other agencies	14

[a] See explanation in Appendix A concerning coverage of tenure tables and computation of tenure and medians. The bases for these percentages are "persons in position" units for each department or type of agency, that is, the number of persons appointed (or reappointed) as political executives to a given position in a given agency. These bases are the same figures as those in Appendix Table C.3, minus 6 persons who were reappointed to discontinuous terms in the same positions (4 in State and 1 each in Post Office and the Federal Communications Commission).

TABLE F.5. *Percentages of Federal Political Executives with Two Years or Less, over Three Years, and over Four Years of Agency Tenure, Ranked by Agency* [a]

Two Years or Less		Over Three Years (Inverse Ranking)		Over Four Years (Inverse Ranking)	
Commerce	57%	Defense	22%	Defense	13%
Defense	53	Commerce	25	Commerce	17
State	48	Air Force	29	State	18
Army	44	HEW	33	Navy	22
All departments	41	State	36	HEW	25
Treasury	40	*All departments*	40	*All departments*	26
Air Force	39	Army	40	Air Force	26
Navy	38	Labor	43	Army	26
Labor	36	Treasury	44	Labor	29
Agriculture	35	Agriculture	46	Treasury	31
Post Office	34	Post Office	47	Interior	32
HEW	33	Justice	50	Justice	33
Interior	32	Navy	53	Agriculture	38
Justice	32	Interior	59	Post Office	41
Emergency agencies	66	Emergency agencies	18	Emergency agencies	8
All agencies	52	*All agencies*	29	*All agencies*	14
Other agencies	46	Other agencies	34	Other agencies	17

[a] See explanation in Appendix A concerning coverage of tenure tables and computation of tenure and medians. The bases for the individual department percentages are "persons in agency" units, that is, the number of persons who served as political executives in that department. The base for "all departments" is the sum of such units. (Example: Henry A. Wallace, who served in both Agriculture and Commerce, is counted once in the base for each of those departments, but twice in the base for "all departments.") The base for "other agencies" and "emergency agencies" is the number of persons who served in such agencies plus 3, because 3 persons served in two agencies (one of which cannot be considered the predecessor of the other) in the "other agencies" or "emergency agencies" categories. The base for "all agencies" is the sum of the units used in "other agencies" and "emergency agencies."

TABLE F.6. *Percentages of Federal Political Executives with Two Years or Less, over Three Years, and over Four Years of Government Tenure, Ranked by Agency* [a]

Two Years or Less		Over Three Years (Inverse Ranking)		Over Four Years (Inverse Ranking)	
Commerce	51%	Defense	29%	State	20%
Defense	47	HEW	33	Defense	22
State	44	Commerce	34	HEW	25
Treasury	38	Air Force	36	Commerce	26
All departments	36	State	37	Air Force	29
Army	35	All departments	46	Labor	31
Labor	33	Agriculture	46	Navy	31
HEW	33	Labor	48	All departments	32
Agriculture	32	Post Office	49	Interior	32
Justice	31	Army	49	Justice	34
Interior	30	Justice	50	Agriculture	40
Air Force	29	Treasury	51	Army	40
Post Office	28	Interior	62	Treasury	40
Navy	22	Navy	64	Post Office	45 ·
Emergency agencies	57	Emergency agencies	32	Emergency agencies	16
All agencies	45	All agencies	39	All agencies	23
Other agencies	40	Other agencies	43	Other agencies	27

[a] See explanation in Appendix A concerning coverage of tenure tables and computation of tenure and medians. The bases for all these percentages are the numbers of persons who served as political executives in the particular department (or type of agency). Each person is counted only once in each department (or type of agency) and only once in each subtotal.

TABLE F.7. *Reappointment of Commissioners by Presidents of the Same and of the Opposite Political Party, by Commission*

| Commission | No Re-appointments | Reappointments | | | Number of Persons |
		Total[a]	President, Same Party	President, Opposite Party	
All seven	59%	41%	38%	6%	203
Civil Aeronautics Board	63	37	30	11	27
Federal Communications Commission	63	37	34	6	35
Federal Power Commission	56	44	44	—	23
Federal Trade Commission	75	25	25	—	24
Interstate Commerce Commission	39	61	57	18	28
National Labor Relations Board	68	32	28	4	25
Securities and Exchange Commission	51	49	46	2	41

[a] Some commissions were reappointed by Presidents of both parties, so the total column may not be the sum of the other two.

154

TABLE F.8. *Total Appointments and Reappointments of Commissioners, by Commission*

Appointments and Reappointments	All Commissions	Civil Aeronautics Board	Federal Communications Commission	Federal Power Commission	Federal Trade Commission	Interstate Commerce Commission	National Labor Relations Board	Securities and Exchange Commission
Partial term only	62	13	9	4	10	6	6	14
1 partial plus 1 reappointment	44	5	10	3	3	6	1	16
1 partial plus 2 reappointments	16	2	2	2	3	5	2	—
1 partial plus 3 reappointments	4	1	—	—	—	2	—	1
1 partial plus 4 reappointments	2	—	—	1	—	2	—	—
1 partial plus 5 reappointments	2	—	—	1	—	1	—	—
1 full term only	57	4	13	9	8	5	11	7
1 full term plus 1 reappointment	18	2	1	5	—	2	5	3
1 full term plus 2 reappointments	6	—	—	1	1	4	—	—
1 full term plus 3 reappointments	1	—	—	—	1	—	—	—
Total persons in commission	212	27	35	25	26	33	25	41

TABLE F.9. *Comparison of Terms of Appointment of Commissioners, Herring Study and Present Study* [a]

Terms to Which Appointed	Herring Study (1887–1935)		Present Study (1933–1965)	
	ICC	*FTC*	*ICC*	*FTC*
Unexpired vacancy	*27%*	*41%*	*28%*	*40%*
Full term	*44*	*53*	*35*	*40*
Second full term	*19*	*6*	*20*	*12*
Third full term	*6*	—	*12*	*5*
Fourth full term	*3*	—	*4*	*2*
Fifth full term	*1*	—	*1*	—
Not reappointed to full term after filling unexpired vacancy	*13*	*22*	*8*	*25*
Number of appointments	86	32	78[b]	40[b]

[a] Percentages may not add to 100 because of rounding.
[b] The numbers here are slightly higher than those in other tables by appointment, because appointments or reappointments before 1933 are counted here for those who are included because of later Roosevelt reappointments.

TABLE F.10. *Method of Termination of Commissioners' Service, by Commission* [a]

Commission	Not Reappointed at End of Term	Resigned Before End of Term	Died in Office	Compulsory Retirement at 70	Number of Persons in Agency
All seven	38%	51%	9%	2%	172
Civil Aeronautics Board	36	64	—	—	22
Federal Communications Commission	41	48	7	3	29
Federal Power Commission	57	24	19	—	21
Federal Trade Commission	43	43	14	—	21
Interstate Commerce Commission	30	44	17	9	23
National Labor Relations Board	65	35	—	—	20
Securities and Exchange Commission	14	80	6	—	36

[a] Percentages may not add to 100 because of rounding.

APPENDIX G

Tables for Chapter 5

TABLE G.1. *Subsequent Careers, by Administration* [a]

Occupation	Administration					
	All Five	Roosevelt	Truman	Eisenhower	Kennedy	Johnson
Still in office April 30, 1965	13%	—	1%	5%	37%	68%
Federal service	18	34%	18	18	26	12
Retired or died	12	14	13	13	2	—
Returned to same organization	21	11	21	28	18	11
Returned to business related to federal executive work	3	1	2	6	2	—
Returned to business unrelated to federal executive work	5	6	5	6	2	1
New in business, related to federal executive work	3	3	2	4	1	—
New in business, unrelated to federal executive work	2	2	3	2	2	—
Same profession, new organization	15	18	22	11	8	7
New profession	3	4	4	3	1	—
Other private	3	4	5	4	1	1
Total private business and professions	55	51	64	63	35	20
Other	2	3	3	1	2	1
Number of persons [b]	984	254	299	341	184	142

[a] Percentages may not add to 100 because of rounding. See Appendix A for a detailed explanation of tabulations of subsequent careers.
[b] Numbers of persons in individual administrations do not add to the total for all administrations, because a person is counted once in each administration he served, but only once in the total for all five administrations.

TABLE G.2. *Subsequent Careers, by Agency* [a]

Agency	Still in Office	Federal Service	Retired or Died	Returned to Same Organization	Business[b] Returned Related	Returned Unrelated	New Related	New Unrelated	Same Profession, New Organization	New Profession	Other Private	Total Private[b]	Other	Number of Persons[c]
All departments, agencies, and commissions	13%	18%	12%	21%	3%	5%	3%	2%	15%	3%	3%	55%	2%	984
State	10	43	9	13	2	5	—	2	9	5	2	38	2	129
Treasury	11	18	7	31	4	4	4	—	16	—	2	61	4	55
Defense	11	11	8	42	6	5	3	—	8	5	—	69	—	62
Army	4	17	11	33	7	15	—	2	9	2	—	68	—	46
Navy	13	8	18	26	5	8	—	3	15	—	3	60	3	39
Air Force	12	12	6	36	6	6	12	3	3	3	—	69	—	38
Justice	9	30	—	19	—	1	1	—	36	1	2	60	1	94
Post Office	14	20	14	12	2	10	—	8	8	—	6	46	6	50
Interior	13	18	13	26	—	3	3	—	21	3	—	56	3	39
Agriculture	13	26	8	15	3	3	—	3	3	5	18	50	5	39
Commerce	8	19	6	31	5	11	3	—	9	2	6	67	—	64
Labor	15	18	10	23	5	3	3	3	10	5	5	57	3	40
HEW	7	22	7	30	—	—	4	—	15	—	4	53	11	27

All departments	*11*	*22*	*9*	*24*	*3*	*5*	*2*	*2*	*14*	*3*	*3*	*56*	*2*	674
Emergency agencies	*3*	*24*	*3*	*19*	*2*	*11*	*5*	*2*	*11*	*8*	*6*	*64*	*5*	62
Other agencies	*7*	*26*	*14*	*17*	*2*	*5*	*2*	*4*	*13*	*4*	*3*	*50*	*2*	95
All agencies	*6*	*24*	*10*	*18*	*2*	*8*	*3*	*3*	*12*	*6*	*5*	*57*	*3*	154
All departments and agencies	*11*	*21*	*9*	*23*	*3*	*6*	*2*	*2*	*14*	*3*	*4*	*57*	*2*	798
CAB	*15*	*19*	*4*	*12*	—	*8*	*8*	—	*19*	*8*	*4*	*59*	*4*	26
FCC	*18*	*9*	*27*	*3*	—	—	*12*	*3*	*27*	—	—	*45*	—	33
FPC	*16*	*4*	*32*	*16*	—	—	*4*	*4*	*16*	*4*	*4*	*48*	—	25
FTC	*19*	*19*	*23*	*15*	—	—	—	—	*23*	—	—	*38*	—	26
ICC	*30*	—	*36*	*9*	*3*	—	*3*	—	*15*	—	*3*	*33*	—	33
NLRB	*20*	*16*	*16*	*12*	*8*	*5*	—	*4*	*28*	—	*4*	*48*	—	25
SEC	*13*	*20*	*8*	*18*	*2*	*1*	*3*	*8*	*10*	*5*	*3*	*60*	*3*	40
All commissions	*19*	*12*	*21*	*12*	*2*	*1*	*4*	*3*	*20*	*2*	*2*	*46*	*1*	204

163

a Percentages may not add to 100 because of rounding. See Appendix A for a detailed explanation of tabulations of subsequent careers.
b See a more detailed description of these categories in Table G.1.
c Numbers of persons in individual agency groupings (for example, State, Emergency agencies) do not add to the subtotals (All departments, All commissions) or to the total departments, agencies, and commissions, because a person is counted once in each agency grouping in which he served, but only once in a subtotal or total grouping.

Index

Abegglen, James C., 9n
Acheson, Dean, 8, 42
Administrators, 3, 7; age, 28; later careers, 74; occupational background, 34–35, 46; tenure, 57–59
Age range of appointees, 26–30
Agency for International Development, 65
Agriculture Department appointees: education, 20–21; geographic origin, 12, 14; later careers, 75, 77; number, 7; occupational background, 36; political affiliation, 25; tenure, 63–65
Air Force appointees: education, 19–20; geographic origin, 12, 14; later careers, 75–77; occupational background, 36; tenure, 65, 68
Anderson, Robert B., 8
Appointments: bipartisan, 23–25; multiple, 8; summary, 6–8
Army appointees: education, 19, 21; geographic origin, 14; later careers, 75–77; occupational background, 36; tenure, 65, 68
Assistant secretaries, 3, 7, 25; age, 28–29; later careers, 73–74; occupational patterns, 33–34, 43, 46, 53; political affiliation unknown, 25; tenure, 56–61, 83
Atchison, Clyde B., 28

Bannerman, Graeme, 43
Baptist appointees, 15–16
Bell, David, 4, 42
Bernstein, Marver H., 5n, 6n, 29, 30n, 54n, 81n
Bipartisan appointments, 23–25, 68
Birnbaum, Max, 22n
Brimmer, Andrew F., 1

Brown, Harold, 68
Brucker, Wilber, 43
Budget Bureau, 4, 20, 65
Business background of appointees, 31–41, 50, 53

Cabinet secretaries, 3, 7; age, 28; education, 18; later careers, 73–74; occupational background, 34, 42–43, 46, 53; political affiliations, 25; tenure, 56–60
Campaign contributions, 26
Career employees, appointment of, 41–45, 50–51, 53
Careers: before appointment, 31–53; after appointment, 73–77
Cass, James, 22n
Catholic appointees, 14–16
Celebrezze, Anthony J., 4
Chapman, Oscar, 12, 36n
Chicago, University of, 22–23
Cities, as source of appointees, 9, 12–14
Civil Aeronautics Board appointees, 5; education, 21; later careers, 76–77; occupational background, 40, 43–44, 48; tenure, 69, 71–72
Cohen, Manuel, 44n
Colleges, of appointees, 17–20, 21–23
Collins, Orvis F., 9n
Columbia University, 22–23
Commerce Department appointees: geographic origin, 12, 14; later careers, 75–77; occupational background, 1, 36; tenure, 63–65
Commissioners, regulatory, 3, 7; age, 29–30; bipartisan requirement, 24–25, 68; education, 17–18, 20–21; geographic origin, 12; later careers, 73–75; occupational background,

165